Th

Student
Bollocks

Joseph Gelfer

s u m m e r s d a l e

Summersdale Publishers Ltd
46 West Street
Chichester
West Sussex
PO19 1RP
UK

www.summersdale.com

Printed and bound in the EU.

ISBN 1 84024 330 9

Contents

Chapter One:
Freshers' Week

The first week at university can be an intimidating time. For many it is the first time away from home. If you make mistakes during Freshers' week it could take you until the beginning of the third year to undo them, so take a moment to glance over the following Freshers' rules.

The minute your parents drop you off at your Hall, go straight to the off-licence. Enjoy the sensation of having vast amounts of unchecked booze in your cupboard for the first time. In fact, bugger the books: spend your allowance on establishing a bar to entertain your fellow intellectuals.

Don't make the mistake of thinking you're never going to make any friends and hooking up with anyone who's around. A bad socialising choice in the early days can lead to disastrous long-term consequences. Appearing slightly mysterious and remote in the face of social try-hards will always be a safe bet.

**At the Freshers' Fair
remember the following:**

1. Get as many goodie bags
as possible – there's food
and contraception in them
there Nokia carrier bags!

2. Join a sensible amount of clubs. You need to cover all your bases, cheese and wine, the rowers and probably the green group for your CV in later life.

3. Speak a foreign language? Join the relevant club – two words: booze cruise.

4. Stock up on posters so your brethren can identify what sort of person you are. Newcastle Brown? Bob Marley? X-Files? They all give away heavily encrypted messages.

5. There will be a plant stall at the Freshers' Fair. A plant stall? DO NOT fall into this trap.

Join the student newspaper.
There are free cinema and gig
tickets to be had, plus the earlier
CV bonus. Hint: if you really
fancy yourself, this is where the
University Challenge cont-
enders are usually headhunted.

Go to the bookshop, but DO NOT buy stuff on the reading list. Artsy types should buy books about Myanmar, Zen and the relationship between drugs and creativity. Sciencey types should buy books on fractals and super-string theory.

Frequent yourself with the names and locations of the major bars and clubs in town – this will stand you in good stead with the other cheese and winers. It will also save you from getting lost and the inevitable financially crippling cab ride back home on your first big night out.

Above all, you've got some stealing to do. Do not fear! Students are a loop-hole in the law. We're talking traffic cones, park benches and even prop submarines (if you can break your way into the Drama department).

Clubs, Societies and their Secret Meanings

You'll find a multiplicity of clubs and societies to join, both during the Freshers' Fair and throughout the year. You might think you know what you're getting yourself into, but there are hidden codes behind each group that you may not be aware of …

Rowing and Hockey Clubs –
These are full of elitist types
who want to excel at something
the university values which has
nothing to do with studying.
The great irony about these
people is that while they always
appear fresh-faced and
wholesome for dawn training
sessions, they're always the first
to be vomiting on the floor later
in the union bar.

Skiing Club –

These are a strange breed of folk. Not only do they tend to be incredibly well off, but they have a habit of never being seen in their departments, apart from the first week of term where they show off their tans and toned physiques.

The Student Newspaper and Student Union –
Second to lawyers, these guys are amongst the most power-hungry students on campus. They may well be studying Ecological Sciences or some seemingly harmless subject but they will be the first among your number to push nasty laws through parliament after graduation.

Political parties of all colours –

Generally an unreasonable bunch, these people are subject to one of two personality traits: they are either megalomaniac loons or unquestioningly carrying out their parents' political ambitions.

Role-Playing Societies –
Didn't Dungeons and Dragons go out in 1986? Maybe, but there's a whole host of strange characters who feel the need to role-play. This is home to all those quiet people who you thought did nothing but watch *Robot Wars*. Also a haven for Engineers.

Cheese and Wine Club –

By far the most civilised of all societies, the Cheese and Winers won't expect you to know your rioja from your shiraz, but will expect you to drink excessively and talk about Byron's poetry and the joys of Ancient Greece.

Drama Society –
Oddly, the Drama Society rarely has anyone in it who actually studies drama, as drama students consider it far beneath them. However it *is* full of wannabe luvvies looking for casual sex and an outlet for their personality disorders. Occasionally they actually put on a play, which is always a laugh.

Photography Club –

What can I say? If you're not into the naked body for art's sake, don't go there. Believe me.

Chapter Two:
The Joy of House Sharing

Unfortunately there is never much choice when it comes to the house you end up living in once you're out of Halls, or the people you end up sharing with.

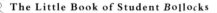
When trawling through the properties on the student accommodation list there are some things to watch out for when considering who you're going to be sharing the kitchen and bathroom with:

• There are patches of jam on the ceiling.

• There are mushrooms in the kitchen – and they're not left over from last night's pizza delivery.

• There are peepholes drilled in the bathroom wall by the next-door neighbour.

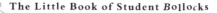

• There are newspapers from 1993 piled up in the hallway – many with letters cut out of the headlines.

• On first inspection you think the wallpaper is anaglypta, but it's actually a random pattern of fluffy mould.

• The grouting in the bathroom looks like it's made of twiglets.

• The mattress is stained in ways that just aren't natural.

• The landlord looks like a hillbilly out of *Deliverance*.

• Next-door's cat likes to hang out there, not because he's friendly, but because of the rodents.

Dodgy student accommodation pales into insignificance compared to weird housemates. Telltale signs that you have moved in with the housemate from hell:

• There's a jam jar full of toenails on the kitchen table.

• They DJ at a thrash-metal club.

• They're pursuing a hobby in taxidermy.

• They have a habit of eating raw meat.

• They have converted their bedroom into a 'war room'.

• They study Engineering.

• They refer to their parents as 'mama' and 'papa'.

Chapter Three:
Living Essentials

Much like a wilderness survival kit, there are various things essential to any student braving Halls.

Be the first person to have a complete kit and the first to realise what nonsense it all is and end up shopping at Ikea.

Some dos:

Pretentious second-hand books (the creases make them look read).

A bong from the local ethnic tat shop – pretend you bought it in Laos.

A tiny mobile phone for texting in a theatrical manner.

A selection of obscure foreign spirits – these will make you look well-travelled and no one will ever drink them.

CDs by unknown bands – this makes you look ahead of your time.

A musical instrument – no one will suspect you can't play it.

A huge bag of lentils so there's always some food in the house.

A top-end games console for bribing new friends.

A swish cookbook to give the right impression (and a hidden student cookbook so you can finally learn how to boil an egg).

A smart pair of sunglasses for shielding hung-over eyes.

Medical kit for UPIs (unidentified pissed injuries) and 'student flu'.

Some don'ts:

Cuddly toys – not even for girls.

Comedy quilt covers.

Star Trek posters.

Hot water bottles and slippers.

Diaries – they *will* get read by others.

Oversized inflatable fruit – not even Engineers find these funny.

43

The Little Book of Student *Bollocks*

Photos of girl/boyfriends at
other universities.

Novelty CDs – last year's
Benidorm anthem just isn't the
same in Sheffield.

The Student Chef

Chances are this will be the first time you've ever really had to cook for yourself. Despite what you see on TV, becoming a culinary expert is relatively simple. Check out some of these items in the classic undergraduate menu.

Spaghetti
with Brussels sprouts.

Spaghetti
with chicken/meat/vegetable
pies.

Spaghetti
with chicken Kiev.

Spaghetti
with chips.

Spaghetti
with ketchup/brown sauce.

All of the above but with
regular pasta instead of
spaghetti.

Fish-finger sarnies.

Crisp sarnies.

Burger sarnies.

Ketchup/brown sauce sarnies.

Sausage sarnies.

Cereal.

Toast
(stale bread made palatable).

Kebabs, pizzas, curries and
Chinese takeaways.

Leftovers of the above.

Accompany all the above
dishes with Tango or Bulgarian
country wine.

Looking After Yourself

After all that junk food you're
going to have to give your poor
old body a chance to recover.
This needn't mean giving up
on your favourite nibbles and
tipples, simply balance them
out by making sure all the food
groups are represented in your
diet and that you raise your
heart rate at least once a day
with some kind of exercise.

Run to the kebab shop instead of strolling lazily.

Race your mates in super-market trollies.

Do reps using 3-litre bottles of cider to improve upper body strength.

Have a marathon yo-yo competition.

Make sure you get all the fruit you need to stay healthy: consume jam, alcopops, ice lollies and wine gums.

Tidy up maniacally after necking handfuls of amphetamines.

Get all the vegetables you need in Pot Noodles and dehydrated camping food.

Go car surfing.

Bypass food altogether with Slimfast and vodka.

Embark upon a very long pub crawl to increase endurance.

Have a high speed mooning tournament.

Chase pigeons – it's fun and aerobic.

Carry all your dirty underwear to the launderette.

Verbally abuse a local and run for your life.

If you're *really* serious about a workout, clean the toilet.

Chapter Four:
Student Spending

Being a student requires thinking like a mini Chancellor of the Exchequer. Even before you've splashed out on being a socialite and gourmet wizard you're going to have to find ways of making the few pounds you do have stretch to the max. Follow these essential tips and you can't go far wrong.

Control your bowel movements so that you don't use your own toilet. By using the bogs at your local pub or shopping mall you can save pounds on loo paper. If you can't make that work, use these public conveniences anyhow and take some paper home with you.

Why spend vast amounts of money on laundry costs? After wearing clothes, simply fold them up and put them away again. Their neat appearance will give the impression of cleanliness. Alternatively, just hang dirty clothes out of the window for a few hours until they smell cleaner.

Why photocopy books at the library when you can simply tear out the relevant pages? No one really reads these dusty old tomes anyhow. The pages of *this* book are, however, electronically tagged …

If you're a guy, sell your sperm. You could argue that this is money-making rather than money-saving – but just think of the free porn.

Instead of buying expensive booze, use the old decanting method. Pour budget wine and spirits into more expensive looking bottles procured from the recycling bins of your local supermarket.

Become a good Samaritan and help out at the city soup kitchen – not forgetting your own healthy portions (also handy for putting on your CV).

Stop eating during the week. It's overrated anyhow.

Take sleeping tablets before going to the pub. You'll wake up the next morning having not spent a penny.

Why buy drugs when you can make them? The Internet is full of cunning ways to get hammered using 10 bananas and a jar of coffee.

Borrow your dad's toolbox and hook yourself up to a neighbour's cable TV. Don't worry about electric shocks – what do you think circuit breakers are for?

Chapter Five:
Sex on Campus

University is a squalid den of vice – if you're lucky. Sexual relations will never be as hassle-free as these few blissful years. However, this doesn't mean you should go for anyone you can get your hands on: be savvy and make nooky work for you as well as being fun.

Be aware of 'beer goggle syndrome' in which potential partners become increasingly attractive as the evening progresses and more drinks are consumed. If you want some but can't stand the prospective lovely, beer goggles can work in your favour. Conversely, if you're not really in the market for any action, you might find that beer goggles bring nothing but trouble.

Oddly, foreign types seem to do disproportionately well when it comes to sexual relations. With this in mind it may be useful to adopt a strange accent and pretend you're from more exotic climes. Remember to adopt a citizenship whose language no one will be fluent in – Hungarian, for example.

Don't shag your flatmate on the first night: you'll have a year to deal with the awkward silences.

Sex with people in positions of influence is never a bad idea. People with powerful jobs in the union will always have lots of free tickets to gigs. If you're a heavier hitter, a little background research may prove useful in finding partners whose parents have handy holiday homes for skiing.

To really throw the cat among the pigeons, try pulling one of the curious breed of mature students in your department. A weird vibe, but bringing with it a certain gravitas.

Sex with a lecturer is a controversial business. Many lecturers have had past secret affairs with students and a leopard never changes its spots. This is a slightly obvious game for female students, but gents could do well by being Dr Love's research assistant for the spring term.

Cleanliness among students is best kept to a minimum. If your drunken fumblings end in a crisply ironed pair of underpants you will do nothing but cause suspicion in the mind of your potential conquest.

It has been known for two scientists to get it together – warning! This could result in a science:science offspring. It is the duty of every arts student to take a scientist on board to prevent this from happening. Scientists already have a big enough cross to bear and cannot be relied on in this matter.

Chapter Six:
Student Archetypes

Unfortunately it is almost impossible to be a student without falling into one of the numerous student archetypes. The very act of seeking individualism pigeon-holes you as 'the Arts Student' (see below). At the very least, make sure you know which pigeon-hole to slot everyone else in.

The Arts Student –

This person is generally highly pretentious but luckily exists in a world where such behaviour is rewarded. Prone to temper tantrums, this person will always make their feelings felt and wear their heart on their sleeve. Subcategories include skaters, ravers, tree-huggers and bookworms.

The Science Student –

This person is highly nerdy but luckily also exists in a world where such behaviour is rewarded. This person will define a hot curry as a wild night out. Subcategories include metallers, athletes and geology society members.

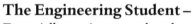

The Engineering Student – Essentially a science student but with a practical chip on their shoulder. Engineering students are the most likely out of the whole student body to wear drain-pipe jeans, white socks and Korn t-shirts. Due to their department being almost solely made up of guys, these fellas congregate in large cliques which would be impenetrable should anyone ever care enough to bother trying. No identified subcategories – no one has yet bothered to look.

The Medical Student –

The scariest student in the university. At some point in the future your life will be in their hands. Just look at them! Generally responsible for some of the most juvenile antics on campus, these guys are rarely aware of any other university department. Subcategories include nurse fetishists and those with a Messiah complex.

The Law Student –

Pretty similar to the medic but more smug as they know that they will earn more in their first job than any other graduate will by the age of 35. Subcategories include would-be politicians, money-hoarders and cheats.

The Modern Languages Student –

These people have the unfair reputation of being the most promiscuous people on campus (this title rightly belongs to the drama department). This person is something of a misfit in the student world, redeemed only by the fact they get a year off in Milan or some equally exotic place. Subcategories include professional secretaries, diplomats and the extraordinarily wealthy.

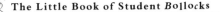

The Drama Student –

These students do not really want to be part of the university as they feel they should be at a separate institution for the performing arts. This person is often highly unstable and prone to extravagant gestures in the name of art. Subcategories include tarts, alcoholics and the depressed.

What Are You Drinking?

This is where you get to either confirm or subvert which student archetype you really are. The drink you swill at the bar is a crucial signifier of the kind of person you are, or want to be. Take note, and cancel that white-wine spritzer …

Lager –

Generally Engineering students, perhaps Medics. They'll be drinking it on a jolly after a rugby or hockey match. Loud and obnoxious, these are the first students to get their hair cut and don a suit after finals.

Bitter –

Often Historians, or one of the other old-school arts subjects that are obscure enough to require retraining as an accountant in later years. These are generally quiet types who look knowingly upon the hoi polloi.

Guinness/Stout –

Welcome to the strange world of the Physicist and the Mathematician. No one has yet figured out the reasoning behind this phenomenon. These drinkers are prone to making jokes about super-string theory.

Cider –
This is a multi-departmental pint which divides its users down the middle. One half of cider drinkers are fresh as daisies and getting drunk for the first time away from home. The other half are hardened drinkers who've been knocking back the White Lightening since the age of 14 and now are revelling in their creative nihilism (generally drama students).

Alcopops –

Clearly any man seen drinking these should be avoided at all costs. However, it is common to observe female Foreign Language students clutching hold of the table while shouting 'I can't feel anything yet!'

Tequila –

This is someone who just can't wait for a pint to kick in. This person will often be the life of the party at the beginning of the night but often falls by the wayside well before first light.

Neat spirits –

This person has probably just got a first look at their reading list and realised that A-levels must indeed be getting easier. May also be suffering from the early knowledge that their boy/girlfriend who went to another university has already been unfaithful.

Mixed spirits –

This is a variation on the Alcopop drinker who is too embarrassed to drink Alcopops. Generally female medics, these drinkers can turn out to be dangerously psychopathic.

Water –

The student drinking water is totally overdrawn, skint and desperate. Freak.

Chapter Seven:
In the Classroom

Apparently some students actually go to seminars and lectures. This shouldn't be seen as simply a dull waste of time, as there is plenty of room for easy self-advancement (other than the obvious gaining of knowledge).

Suss out your personal tutor – you're stuck with this one for years. If you're as smart as a blade, don't let on yet or they'll want to pull you down in your first year. If you're comfortable with being average, show it – they love a good honest hard worker.

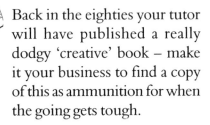

Back in the eighties your tutor will have published a really dodgy 'creative' book – make it your business to find a copy of this as ammunition for when the going gets tough.

You know by now if you're any good at exams. This is never going to change, so don't kid yourself. Choose the right course to suit your slackability rating.

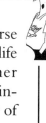

Be mindful of which course subjects you choose. In later life they have to be either marketable or mad, never in-between. So ditch 'History of the Victorian Novel' and opt for 'Databases for Call Centres' or 'Nose Flutes of New Guinea Pygmies' (they're both something to talk about during interviews).

Seen a cute lecturer? Go for it! It can make a dull class quite bearable.

Give the impression that you're well organised intentions by using vast amounts of coloured folder dividers and plastic wallets. Employ a fake numbering system on the spine of the folder to make it look like you have more than one folder per course.

Always refer to at least one book that's not on the reading list: this makes it look like you've read all the others and found them insufficient.

Learn some technical jargon for cunning footnotes: one *ibid.* is equal in marking to two new references.

Make sure you pay regular visits to the library. There is much dating potential here and plenty of opportunities for eye-contact and footsie.

No one is fooled by people who photocopy hundreds of pages from books in the library – save your money for coffees and booze.

Never assume that everyone else is smarter than you – they've just read a book like this one.

Chapter Eight:
About Town

Remember, you are the university representative off campus. The way you behave reflects not only on yourself, but the university at large. Bollocks! Assimilating yourself into your new home town is the fastest way of shaking off geekiness.

When it comes to finding a new place to live, do not skimp! A cool flat will bring much kudos and better populated parties.

Avoid like the plague all the inexcusably dull people you met at the clubs you signed up for at the Freshers' Fair.

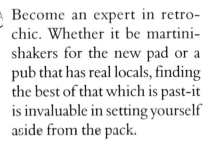

Become an expert in retro-chic. Whether it be martini-shakers for the new pad or a pub that has real locals, finding the best of that which is past-it is invaluable in setting yourself aside from the pack.

Be seen about town looking into purchasing plane tickets to exotic places. Casually discarded flight itineraries, which come free of charge, are almost as good as getting out the photos.

If you have to get a job, NEVER get one in a pub – serving beers to drunk people you probably don't particularly like is the worst thing in the world.

Make sure you get to know a few shady characters – but not too well.

Never pay your TV licence as a matter of principle.

Be nice to the bank and always pay them a visit on the way *to* the pub rather than on the way *back* from it. When applying for an overdraft you will need to quadruple the amount of money you spend on food to make the sums look acceptable.

At some point you will end up at a party at a tutor's house - DO NOT under any circumstances try and snog their children, even if they are your age and unfathomably attractive given their parentage.

Chapter Nine:
Cunning Revision and Exam Tips

Doing well at the end of year exams is not just about being clever – it's about being smart. There's no need to sweat blood over this part of the year – the real smart cookie has a few tricks up the sleeve to smooth the way of this potentially stressful time.

• Surround yourself with seriously clever swots. You can absorb some of their knowledge by osmosis, as well as by borrowing their notes.

• Revise with attractive study partners – it's amazing how much easier it is to spend endless dark hours with a cute person.

• Download essays from the Internet – the Yanks have been at it for years, but don't forget you need Anglicized (*oops*, Anglicised) spellings.

• Always have a couple of drinks before going into the exam hall – most creative genius is born out of being squiffy.

• Make a collage of celebrity stunners and have interesting facts emanating from their lips in speech bubbles (e.g., Brad Pitt: 'The rule of Charlemagne was crucial to the development of the Church'; Julia Roberts: 'Alpha series is absolutely convergent if beta series is conditionally convergent').

• Etch various calculus formulae or Sanskrit quotes into your pencil wood (i.e., cheat) – preferably something relevant to the paper you're about to sit.

• An eccentric rant of an essay about nothing in particular is always better than a feeble essay about the actual question being asked. Give the impression you're painting on a broader canvas.

• Try and avoid circling the tops of i's and j's or drawing happy faces after points you're particularly proud of.

• Writing in mauve or green ink does not make you look more creative – more that you have learning difficulties.

• Rest assured that no one will ever ask to see your degree certificate, so if you do end up with a crap mark just say you got a 2:1.

Chapter Ten:
The Summer Holidays

What you get up to in the summer holidays reflects upon your reputation during term time. In fact, the holidays are often the best part of the university year. So that you can read between the lines in the bar come October, here's a little translation guide to holiday activities.

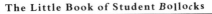

I spent my time catching up with family
– *I stayed at home.*

I developed my work experience skills to boost my CV on graduation
– *I spent two months working in a pet-food factory.*

Yeah man, I travelled around India meeting some really spiritual people
– *I stayed in a cockroach-infested hotel in Delhi and got the runs.*

I worked on a volunteer project in South America
– *I paid someone £400 so I could clean up plastic bags for people who didn't really want me there.*

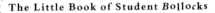

I really got into horticulture
– *This term I will be supplementing my student loans by selling vast amounts of homegrown weed.*

I worked extensively on my dissertation
– *I'm heading for a nervous breakdown.*

What holiday?
– *I've been taking too many drugs.*

We should stop stealing park benches
– *I've just been released from a three-month stretch inside after that stunt at the end of last term.*

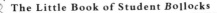

I learned to sail
— *The parents of that foreign languages student I pulled at the end of term party owned a yacht moored at St Tropez.*

The Little Book of Student Bollocks

Chapter Eleven:
The Real World

Sooner or later you're going to have to think about life after graduation. This is a time to take stock of what you're good at, and then put a spin on it to make is socially constructive.

I have a good understanding of law
– I got away with TV licence and council tax evasion, not to mention theft of numerous street signs.

I use my initiative to do whatever's necessary to get the job done
– I downloaded essays from the internet and passed them off as my own.

122

I developed my own form of 'fusion cuisine'
– *I was the first person in town to ever combine spaghetti with chicken pies.*

My favourite time of day is early morning
– *Just before I go to bed.*

I'm strongly committed to the idea of recycling
– *If you turn your socks inside out you can wear them for a second day.*

I know the importance of prioritising tasks
– *I always leave the washing-up until the end of the week.*

Health is of paramount importance to me
– *I always smoke low-tar cigarettes.*

EMMA
BURGESS

THE LITTLE BOOK OF
**ESSENTIAL
FOREIGN
SWEAR
WORDS**

summersdale *humour*

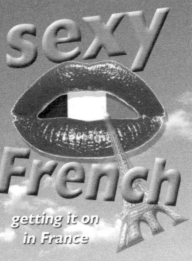

sexy

French

getting it on in France

Emma Burgess

summersdale *humour*

THE LITTLE BOOK OF
CHAT-UP LINES
Are your legs tired? You've been running through my mind all day.
Yeah, I was looking for a brain cell.
STEWART FERRIS
summersdale humour

For the latest humour books from Summersdale, check out

www.summersdale.com

Chicago

Select

contents

Chicago overview

Exuding a unique combination of Midwest charm and big-city sophistication, Chicago welcomes visitors to its spindly, glittery skyline with open arms. From its picturesque lakefront and cultural, shopping, and nightlife gems to its diverse neighborhoods and world-class dining, the US's 'second city' consistently proves itself to be a first-rate destination.

Chicago is renowned for a number of things: its landmark museums, iconic architecture, and influential comedy, theater, and blues scenes. Exploring these is rightly high up the 'to-do' list of most visitors, but while these attractions are significant and the scenes ever-vibrant, they aren't necessarily what defines the city as a whole.

In Chicago, urban and local farms supply fresh bounty year-round, the underground music scene is lively, and politics – for better or worse – sparks talk far beyond city limits. Forward-thinking boutiques blend with galleries; quaffs can be had from any number of moody, destination-

worthy lounges, dive bars, or city-center breweries; and the harsh winter is no deterrent to enjoying nature at the many indoor and outdoor gardens. In fact, many locals appreciate the winters, as they make the summers feel all the more luscious.

The best way to experience Chicago is to approach it like a local. Veer away from the tourist traps and instead tackle the hometown heroes and must-sees from an off-kilter vantage point. Make fast tracks for the city's emergent hotspots to see first-hand the role that under-the-radar designers, artists, and musicians play in giving Chicago such a depth of allure. And take advantage of the numerous free experiences that the city offers, from outdoor concerts and stunning public sculptures to walking through the parks and markets, or catching some rays at the beach. Meanwhile, whatever you do, dine out often; Chicago is famed for its fabulous food, found across the spectrum from haute haunts to mom-and-pop restaurants to casual stands.

Finally, don't forget to ascend to the city's highest reaches, drinking in the amazing views out over this architectural playground that has sprung from the prairies.

in the mood for...

... a quintessential experience

There's a time and a place to blend in with locals. There's also a time to do what visitors do best: see and experience just what gives Chicago iconic appeal. At **The Second City Training Center** in Old Town (*p.48*), sketch comedy and writing classes give comedians-in-training the last laugh. Nearby, splurge-seekers meet their match when meandering the **Magnificent Mile** (*p.62*), the city's signature upscale shopping and dining strip. Consider catching a baseball game – either the Cubs at **Wrigley Field** (*p.29*) or the White Sox at **U.S. Cellular Field** (*p.140*) – and grabbing a slice from **The Art of Pizza** (*p.26*). Alternatively, head to **Navy Pier** to see the near-hidden **Smith Museum of Stained Glass** (*p.74*) or visit the year-round **Chicago Shakespeare Theater** (*p.82*), a courtyard-style performance venue dedicated to the works of its namesake.

... a slice of history

From the onset, Chicago has been a resourceful and innovative – not to mention resilient – city. Rising from the ashes of the Great Chicago Fire, it went on to host the World's Columbian Exposition of 1893 at **Jackson Park** *(p.144)* and the Midway Plaisance. Learn about its rich roots at the **Chicago History Museum** *(p.81)*, or **Bronzeville Information Center** *(p.143)*, or take a gangster-themed tour with **Weird Chicago** *(p.76)*.

... bar-hopping

Make like the locals and get a drink in – the options are as plentiful as the scenes are diverse. At retro-feeling **Weegee's Lounge** *(p.111)*, classic cocktails prevail. Meanwhile, house-brewed craft beer reigns at **Revolution Brewing** *(p.119)* and sophisticated sips – incorporating house-made bitters, syrups, and customized ice – set a sedate tone at **The Violet Hour**, a culinary cocktail bar for sophisticates *(p.111)*. Alternatively, there's always Little Italy, where **Davanti Enoteca** *(p.132)* proffers cost-conscious quartinos of wine from a refurbished barn wood bar.

... retail therapy

Shopping opportunities abound in Chicago, whether it's board games from **Cat & Mouse Game Store** (*p.112*) you seek, fashion finds from stylish **Oak Street** (*p.69*), or local labels from **Cerato** (*p.30*). For a different experience, swing by **The Denim Lounge** (*p.77*), where countless cuts all-but-ensure the perfect fit, or discover throwback fashions in the Ukrainian Village and Wicker Park, where stores such as **Dovetail**, **Very Best Vintage**, and **Kokorokoko** nod to eras past (*p.108*). If clothes aren't your thing, never fear. Funky cool plants lure enthusiasts to modern-minded **Sprout Home** (*p.115*), a sleek source for tillandsia, fairy-like indoor gardens, and outdoor habitats. Meanwhile, bookworms can revel in three-story **Myopic Books** (*p.110*) in the Wicker Park neighborhood, which is crammed with over 80,000 editions, many used. For music-lovers, the impressive selection of new and used tunes from **Reckless Records** (*p.117*) holds plenty of appeal.

8

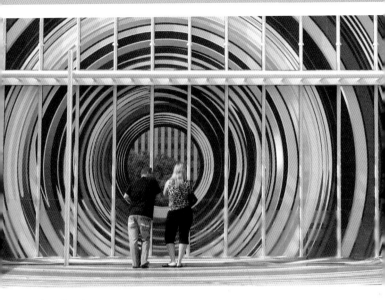

... a tête-à-tête

Peruse the fab collection, hand-in-hand, at the **Modern Wing** at the **Art Institute of Chicago** *(p.91)*, a pristine, whitewashed space designed by architect Renzo Piano. After lunching at Tony Mantuano's **Terzo Piano** within, sneak into **Eno** *(p.75)* – nestled just off of the Magnificent Mile in the posh Intercontinental Chicago. Intimate and approachable, it's a fave for canoodling couples who appreciate fruits of the vine. Or, consider veering toward **WaterShed** *(p.72)*, an intimate, sleek cocktail parlor beneath bubbly bar Pops for Champagne.

Once settled in, try cocktails made from artisanal Great Lakes' spirits, local craft beers, and regional wines. When the weather cooperates, follow that with a walk through the **Lurie Garden** in Millennium Park, or wind down at an outdoor concert featuring **Grant Park Orchestra & Chorus** *(p.88)*, which puts on a free, seasonal series along Chicago's lakefront. Too chilly? Get tickets for an up-close-and-personal live show with hipsters at **Double Door** *(p.113)*, a bi-level bar and concert venue at the bustling crossroads of North, Damen, and Milwaukee Avenues.

... a gourmet blow-out

It is no secret that Chicago is a destination for food lovers – there really is something for everyone and every budget. Whether you crave cutting-edge haute cuisine or the perfect sandwich, Chicago delivers in spades.

Those who want something simple made by a star chef should begin (or end) a day at **XOCO** (p.78), where Rick Bayless protégés turn out churros and fresh-brewed cocoa in the morning, followed by wood-burning oven-crisped *tortas* and soothing, chili-blaced *caldos* (soups) later on. True splurges, though, are had at the famous **Charlie Trotter's** in Lincoln Park (p.50) and nearby **Alinea** (p.50), Grant Achatz's world-renowned dining destination, where deconstructed, artistic edibles provoke thought. If you're without a life savings to spend, however, hit the chefs' budget-friendly alternatives instead, such as swanky carry-out **Trotter's To Go** (p.50) or **Seven on State** (p.97), Macy's food court with a celebrity chef difference.

Another way to indulge royally without going broke is at **Jam** (p.116), a contemporary, cost-conscious brunch destination serving dishes such as malted custard French toast with rhubarb, lime leaf cream, and pink peppercorn, or eggs Benedict with crisped pork belly and beet hollandaise.

For a foodie browse, you can always head to **Green City Market** (p.46), a chef-populated farmers' market with a range of ongoing food-related events, the **Chicago French Market** (p.94) for a curated collection of enticing eats, or the **Maxwell Street**

10

Market (*p.130*), heaven for multicultural bites from Mexican street food to Polish sausages. True connoisseurs of Mexican food should also scurry to **Chilam Balam** (*p.36*) for sustainable, communal plates. For a taste of southeast Asia, visit Uptown's **Argyle Street** (*p.32*), or for under-the-radar Armenian eats hit **Sayat Nova** (*p.69*) in Streeterville. Alternatively, head to **Valois Cafeteria** (*p.142*) on the city's South Side for great soul food.

And when nothing but red meat will do, visit **Johnnie's Beef** (*p.164*) for messy, exemplary Italian sandwiches and all-beef hot dogs.

... enjoying the outdoors

Many vibrant, uniquely Chicago experiences are waiting to be had in the great, wide open. See some of the city's most beloved sights from the water with **Chicago River Canoe and Kayak** (*p.128*) or aboard a **Seadog Cruise** speedboat (*p.71*). Alternatively, jump on a food-centric walking tour with **Chicago Food Planet** (*p.67*) or hop on a bicycle to explore President Obama's neighborhood with **Bobby's Bike Hike** (*p.73*). Of course, you could always make the trip to the **Chicago Botanic Garden** (*p.169*), a four-season beauty with year-round events.

... views from the top

Chicago has no shortage of sky-high views. Among the most hyped – not to mention frequently visited – are the **Hancock Observatory** (*p.62*) and **Skydeck Chicago** (*p.90*), complete with hovering glass-ledge floor in the Willis Tower. For something more stylish, make your way to rooftop **Vertigo Sky Lounge** (*p.65*), a 26th-floor hangout in the Dana hotel and spa, where DJs spin beats and an outdoor patio opens to stunning skyline views – including in winter, when an ice bar turns out warming libations.

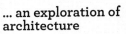

... an exploration of architecture

Chicago is known as an architect's playground and deservedly so. The city is filled with buildings designed by prominent architects and urban planners; examples include the Montauk Building by Daniel Burnham and John Wellborn Root and the Illinois Institute of Technology campus by Ludwig Mies van der Rohe.

See some of the city's structural wonders during the Chicago Architecture Foundation's **Elevated Architecture: Chicago's Loop by Train** tour (*p.93*), or wander past historic gravestones at **Graceland Cemetery** (*p.34*), which is the final resting place of Daniel Louis Sullivan and Willis Tower architect Fazlur Khan.

For something a bit off the beaten path, pay a visit to **Astor Street** (*p.69*) in the Gold Coast, an historic district filled with breathtaking, historical revival homes in varying styles, tucked between 20th-century apartment buildings and townhouses. Or get acquainted with Prairie style structures at the **Robie House** (*p.138*) and **Frank Lloyd Wright Home and Studio** (*p.165*).

... family fun

When traveling with kids, itineraries must include enough stops to keep boredom at bay. Thankfully, there are plenty of tot-friendly destinations that grown-ups can appreciate, too. Take Mexican candy store **Dulcelandia Del Sol** *(p.112)* in Logan Square as a perfect case in point. Trimmed with piñatas, it is jammed with bins and aisles of colorful bulk candies and chocolates, bagged botanas, and pillowy marshmallows.

For a different approach, pay a visit to **Berwyn's Toy Trains & Models** *(p.168)*, where a back room houses a working electric train and covetable toys threaten impulse buys. Continue to the funky finds – retro wind-up robots, kazoos and limited-edition tin trinkets – at **Pumpkin Moon** *(p.168)*.

Alternatively, you could always wile away the day in hands-on fashion at **Kohl Children's Museum** *(p.166)*, home to a play sandwich shop, grocery store and human 'car wash,' followed by scoops at **Homer's Ice Cream** *(p.167)*. Hit Museum Campus to explore sea life at the **John G. Shedd Aquarium** or learn about stars at the **Adler Planetarium** *(p.124)*. Or head for the failsafe (and free) option of the **Lincoln Park Zoo** *(p.49)*.

... a culture fix

Chicago gets labeled a workaday city, but it is also rich with culture and home to many inspiring spots filled with the work of innovators. At the fine arts-focused **Mary and Leigh Block Museum** *(p.169)* on the Northwestern University campus, see traveling exhibits, catch films of note, or peruse its outdoor sculpture garden. At the **Ernest Hemingway Museum and Birthplace Home** *(p.159)*, tour the Queen Anne-style childhood home of the author. Alternatively, explore the **Museum of Contemporary Art** *(p.66)* or the gallery-packed **Chicago Arts District** *(p.127)*.

... an offbeat exploration

There are no rules when it comes to exploring the city and taking the roads less traveled can allow you to get really stuck in. At the **Lillstreet Art Center** *(p.28)*, for example, printmaking and metal-smithing classes are just the tip of the iceberg, while you can build your own 'friends' at **RobotCity Workshop** *(p.33)*. Pay a visit to **Uncommon Ground** *(p.40)*, where you can tour the rooftop garden and see open mic while sampling the goods in the dining room. Or for something that's just for adults, explore the city's raunchier side at **Gallery Provocateur** *(p.114)*.

15

... wee hours entertainment

Dark and gritty with a punky, rock-and-roll aesthetic, **Delilah's** *(p.53)* is a venerable, DePaul area watering hole with 400-plus whiskeys and DJs spinning a great mix of familiar and lesser-known beats, mixed up with a dose of 1990s kitsch. Visit before seeing a show at **Metro** *(p.27)*. This concert venue – located in a former theater – hosts a range of on-the-verge local, regional, and national acts; it also launched the careers of bands such as Smashing Pumpkins and Urge Overkill.

When the timing is right, you could always tip back suds at **The Brew & View** *(p.31)*, when there aren't performances booked. This raucous, alternate persona of the Vic concert hall morphs into a place where double and triple-bill film screenings meet drink specials. (Thankfully, basic bites help ward off hangovers.) From there, move on to wee-hours **Lincoln Karaoke** *(p.38)*. Easy to miss given its strip mall address, this private-room parlor caters to drunken songbirds.

If you're after more of a hipster vibe, check out the live music venues around Wicker Park, such as **Double Door** *(p.113)*, or hit **Coles** *(p.118)* in Logan Square for the open mic night.

... escaping the crowds

Chicago is full of larger-than-life locales and non-stop freneticism. While these attributes give the city its pulse, these same qualities make a bit of respite necessary from time to time. When some quiet is needed, explore the scenic, waterfall-fed pools at the **Osaka Japanese Garden** *(p.145)*, continuing to the Paul Douglas Nature Sanctuary – known colloquially as the **'Wooded Island'** *(p.145)* – a lush, bird-populated paradise. Or don your walking shoes and explore **Washington Park** *(p.143)*, where both the **DuSable Museum of African American History** *(p.149)* and *Fountain of Time* sculpture

by Lorado Taft reside. When the weather won't cooperate, there's always a jungle in the **Lincoln Park Conservatory** *(p.55)*, an exotic, park-centered structure overseen by lush palms and ancient ferns. However, when it's warm, walk further and find the peaceful **Alfred Caldwell Lily Pool** *(p.47)*, where stone paths cut through the woodland landscape.

neighborhoods

Situated on the shores of Lake Michigan, the United States' third-largest city sports 77 distinct, vibrant communities, each offering a different experience to the next. Easy to navigate, the city of Chicago follows a grid system, increasing 100 numbers per block.

Lakeview to Rogers Park Chicago's lake-lined, northernmost reaches have very distinct personalities. The former is home to the Chicago Cubs and supports both a diverse food scene and one of the country's largest, not to mention most thriving, LGBT communities. Meanwhile, the latter exudes charm that's equal parts college town, multicultural enclave, and arts hub.

Lincoln Park and Old Town Perched between the Chicago River and Lake Michigan, Lincoln Park and Old Town comprise some of the city's most scenic and historically notable areas. Filled with natural beauty, they're home to posh boutiques and soaring brownstones set on cobblestone streets, landmark museums, and booming, renowned comedy and theater scenes.

Gold Coast, Magnificent Mile, Streeterville, and River North Home to Chicago's wealthy elite, these neighborhoods – located on the city's near north side – are hotspots for shoppers, bar-goers, and celeb-seekers alike. Dotted with soaring high-rises and iconic architecture, they're also packed with galleries, both fine-dining and budget-friendly restaurants, and lively nightlife options.

The Loop and West Loop There's no denying the allure or ever-present bustle of the skyscraper-laden, centrally located Loop and West Loop districts. Home to a wealth of culture – from eye-popping, revered public art to an underground world and sky-high structures – these districts are also peppered with places to chill out and reflect, soak up the lakefront, or score farm-fresh fare.

Logan Square, Wicker Park, and Ukrainian Village There's much to love about these hipster-populated communities. Located on the city's northwest side, these neighborhoods offer a perfect sojourn for lit-lovers and music fanatics alike, while vintage clothing enthusiasts, foodies, and beer fans will also find their match.

South Loop, Little Italy, Chinatown, and Pilsen From enclaves brimming with enticing ethnic eats, to spots where history comes alive, these near-south districts are poised for adventure. Featuring distinctive Italian, Asian, and Mexican communities, these locales are also the site of off-the-beaten-track museums, rambling parkland, and notable national landmarks.

Hyde Park and the South Side Packed with lauded locales but less-frequented by visitors, Hyde Park and the South Side feel undiscovered but are flush with fab finds, whether you want to learn about African-American history, kick back over live blues, explore the museum campus, or root for the home team at U.S. Cellular Field.

Outlying Neighborhoods Stretching west of the city and encompassing the far north suburbs, Chicago's outlying neighborhoods offer a break from the bustle of downtown and plenty of room to roam. Whether you walk amid sculpture or flowers at a botanic garden, soak up literary and architectural history, or enjoy some all-ages fun, the options are endless.

Chicago

2 miles

2 km

N

Lake Michigan

20

LINCOLN PARK

Theater on the Lake

John Hancock Center

Magnificent Mile

Navy Pier

MILLENNIUM PARK

GRANT PARK

Art Institute of Chicago

Field Museum

Adler Planetarium

Soldier Field

Michigan Avenue

State St

SOUTH LOOP

LOOP

Willis Tower

NEAR NORTH

GOLD COAST

OLD TOWN

Lincoln Park Zoo

Halsted Street

Ohio

W Division St

North

LINCOLN PARK

N. Lake Shore Drive

UPTOWN

LAKEVIEW

Wrigley Field

North

West Addison Street

West Belmont Avenue

West Diversey Avenue

Fullerton Avenue

AVONDALE

ANDERSONVILLE

Ashland Ave

North Lincoln Avenue

Clark Street

Lincoln Avenue

Irving Park

Western Avenue

WICKER PARK

Polish Museum of America

Avenue

North

Grand

United Center

Eisenhower Expressway

LITTLE ITALY

University of Illinois

PILSEN

Ashland Avenue

Damen Avenue

W Randolph

HUMBOLDT PARK

Garfield Park Conservatory

Kedzie Avenue

GARFIELD PARK

Hamlin Blvd

Homan

DOUGLAS PARK

West

South

RAVENSWOOD

West Foster Avenue

Lawrence

Montrose

Chicago

Avenue

IRVING PARK

North Elston Avenue

LOGAN SQUARE

North

North Milwaukee Avenue

Pulaski Road

Avenue

Kimball Avenue

North

West

West

West

AUSTIN

Cicero Avenue

N Laramie Avenue

Washington Blvd

COLUMBUS PARK

Central Avenue

Austin

Kostner Avenue

West

50

Glenview

O'Hare Airport

John F. Kennedy Expressway

POLONIA

HARWOOD HEIGHTS

NORRIDGE

W. Foster Ave

West Irving Park Road

West Montrose Avenue

West Belmont Avenue

Harlem Avenue

Narragansett Avenue

CRAGIN

Diversey Avenue

Fullerton Avenue

50

North Austin Avenue

West Division Street

W Grand Ave

ELMWOOD PARK

RIVER FOREST

OAK PARK

Oak Park Avenue

Frank Lloyd Wright Home and Studio

North Avenue

West Lake Street

64

North Avenue

West

MAYWOOD

FOREST PARK

BERWYN

Ridgeland Ave

S. Austin

West

Roosevelt Road

290

West

43

19

94

90

41

50

43

Burnham Park

Lake Shore Drive

41

Museum of Science and Industry

★ Illinois Institute of Technology

BRONZEVILLE

★ University of Chicago

HYDE PARK

JACKSON PARK

Drexel Blvd

East 47th Street

East 51st Street

WASHINGTON PARK

★ DuSable Museum of African American History

East 63rd Street

East 67th Street

East 71st Street

South Chicago Avenue

East 79th Street

South Stony Island Avenue

CHATHAM

E. 87th Street

E. 95th Street

Chicago Skyway

12 20

90

94

94

Dr Martin Luther King Drive

South Cottage Grove Avenue

South State Street

90 94

Dan Ryan Expressway

S Halsted Street

57

BRIDGEPORT

Pershing Road

South Halsted Street

South

West Pershing

West 51st Street

West Garfield Boulevard

ENGLEWOOD

West 71st Street

75th Street

79th Street

South Ashland Avenue

South Damen Avenue

83rd Street

S Western Avenue

BEVERLY

GAGE PARK

CHICAGO LAWN

West 59th Street

West 63rd Street

West 67th Street

MARQUETTE PARK

ASHBURN

Columbus Avenue

Kedzie Avenue

EVERGREEN PARK

South

HOMETOWN

Archer Avenue

Santa

E. Stevenson Expressway

Adlai

South

West 47th Street

West 55th Street

Chicago Midway Airport ✈

South Cicero Avenue

Central Avenue

West

BEDFORD PARK

South Pulaski Road

50

Cicero Avenue

South

State Street

79th Street

87th Street

95th Street

BURBANK

West

OAK LAWN

Sanitary and Ship Canal

STICKNEY

West Pershing Road

West Ogden Avenue

So

S

FOREST VIEW

★ Chicago Portage National Historic Site

South Archer Avenue

Harlem Avenue

South

Avenue

LYONS

55

Michigan

SUMMIT

43

W. 71st St

BRIDGE-VIEW

West

171

294

21

Lakeview to Rogers Park

Lakeview to Rogers Park

Abiquiu Café C2
Aragon Ballroom C5
The Art of Pizza B1
The Bad Apple A4
Big Jones B6
Cerato C2
Chicago River Canoe and Kayak A2
Chilam Balam D1
First Slice Pie Café B4
Gethsemane Garden Center B7
Giordano's C2
Graceland Cemetery C4
Half Acre Beer Company A4
Hidden Cove Lounge A6
Hutchinson Street C4
Koval Distillery B5
Leather Archives and Museum B8
Lillstreet Art Center B4
Lincoln Karaoke A6
Machu Picchu B3
Merz Apothecary A5
Metro C3
Metropolitan Brewing B5
Murphy's Bleachers C3
Music Box Theatre C3
Nancy's D1
Pho 777 C5
RoboCity Workshop C2
Rosehill Cemetery A7
Sapore di Napoli C2
Schubas Tavern C2
Smart Bar C3
Tigerlilie Salon A5
Uncle Fun C2
Uncommon Ground C8
The Vic C2
Vines on Clark C2
Wrigley Field C3

24

Beach

4 · 3 · 2 · 1

LINCOLN PARK

Montrose Harbor

Belmont Harbor

SYDNEY R. MARAVITZ GOLF CLUB

North Lake Shore Drive

Lake Shore Drive

North Sheridan Raod

Chilam Balam

Nancy's

North Broadway St

West Belmont Avenue

North Clark Street

West Diversey Parkway

North Broadway Street

North Halstead Street

North Halstead Street

North Sheffield Avenue

West Addison Street

LAKEVIEW

Murphy's Bleachers

The Vic

North Sheffield Avenue

Red Line

Metro

Smart Bar

Wrigley Field

RobotCity Workshop

Abiquia Café

Belmont

Wellington

North Racine Avenue

West Irving Park Road

Sheridan

North Sheffield Avenue

North Clark Street

Music Box Theatre

Vines on Clark

North Racine Avenue

Giordano's

North Lincoln Avenue

Diversey

Brown Line

GRACELAND CEMETERY

Uncle Fun

Schubas Tavern

UPTOWN

West Montrose Avenue

North Clark Street

West Waveland Avenue

North

Corato

Southport

Avenue

West Ashland Avenue

Southport

Sapore di Napoli

Lilstreet Art Center and First Slice Pie Café

Machu Picchu

Paulina

The Art of Pizza

North Ravenswood Avenue

North Ravenswood Avenue

Montrose

Brown Line

Irving Park

Addison

WELLES PARK

The Bad Apple

Half Acre Beer Company

North Lincoln Avenue

North Damen Avenue

North Damen Avenue

West Diversey Parkway

HAMLIN PARK

North Clybourn Avenue

West Addison Street

West Irving Park Road

West Addison Street

West Cornelia Avenue

West Rosow Street

West School Street

West Belmont Avenue

North Western Avenue

North Western Avenue

REVERE PARK

Chicago

West Montrose Ave

Chicago River Canoe and Kayak

4 · 3 · 2 · 1

A · B · C · D · E

25

Dive into divine deep-dish with locals – not tourists – at **The Art of Pizza**

Chicago has a near-endless supply of pizza varieties, from coal-fired to wood-burning oven-blistered, a 'potpie'-inspired take, and the cracker-crusted version, which is favored at taverns. Yet few visitors can conceive of a Chicago visit without experiencing deep-dish pizza and the masses flock to chains such as **Pizzeria Uno** (29 E. Ohio Street; tel: 312-321-1000), **Lou Malnati's** (439 N. Wells Street; tel: 312-828-9800), and **Gino's East** (633 N. Wells Street; tel: 312-943-1124). It's understandable, since deep-dish – in all its round, cheesy glory – was invented in the 1940s in Chicago, allegedly by Uno's. The city of Chicago is also credited with the stuffed variant, inspired by Italian Easter pie and made popular by places like **Nancy's** (3970 N. Elson Avenue; tel: 773-267-8182) and **Giordano's** (730 N. Rush Street; tel: 312-951-0747; map C2).

However, these days, **The Art of Pizza** in Lakeview is where locals rightly indulge. After a likely 45 minute wait, dive into hefty, stuffed pizza, served in a bare-bones, sunshine-hued storefront. Playing a starring role is the golden, flaky crust, equal parts crisp and doughy, buttery and dense. Filled with enough gooey mozzarella – and, if you're wise, fennel-laced sausage – to stop one's heart on the spot, it's blanketed in handily seasoned, tangy tomato sauce. A popular, gut-busting alternative is the aptly named 'Art's Meaty Delight,' packed with not just sausage but also bacon, pepperoni, and beef.

Thin-ish crust and pan pies are options, too, along with a roster of foot-long subs, daily specials, and Italian beef, sausage, and meatball sandwiches. If you're on the fly, you can also just grab a slice.

The Art of Pizza; 3033 N. Ashland Avenue; tel: 773-327-5600; Sun–Thur 11am–10.30pm, Fri–Sat 11am–11.30pm; map B1

Catch an **alt-rock show** at **Metro** in Lakeview

Since it rolled out the red carpet in 1982, **Metro** – known colloquially as 'The Metro' and, historically, 'Cabaret Metro' – has spotlighted emerging acts. Many of them, including R.E.M., The Smashing Pumpkins, and Nirvana, appeared back-in-the-day as they were on the cusp of blowing up. So, it stands to reason that if walls could talk, this gritty, independent theater-turned concert venue would have stories to tell. One thing is for sure: it is the site of countless music memories. Long a bastion for Chicago hopefuls – think Big Black and Naked Raygun – it has also welcomed many an overseas band looking to make it in the States, including New Order.

Originally built as a Swedish cultural center in 1927, the pad continues to host recognized and lesser-known performers across the genres today, including big-name musicians who haven't forgotten their roots. For the best view, stake your spot on the balcony, and remember to stop by **Smart Bar** (www.smartbarchicago. com), its divey, lower-level adjunct. This late-night hang out hosts cutting edge and resident DJs – plus the occasional, intimate, after-hours show. Sign up for its mailing list, a resource for advance ticket information; ditto its text sign-up, which provides valuable day-of-show details.

Other locally-beloved live music venues that deserve consideration include **Schubas Tavern** (3159 N. Southport Avenue; tel: 773-525-2508; map C2) and **Double Door** (*p.113*). The newer (and larger) **Lincoln Hall** (2424 N. Lincoln Avenue; tel: 773-525-2501; p.44 map C4), at home in the former 3 Penny Cinema down in Lincoln Park, is from the Schubas crew and is a force to be reckoned with, too.

Metro; 3730 N. Clark Street; tel: 773-549-4140; metrochicago.com; various dates and times; charge; map C3

Coax your inner artist – whatever your age – at
Lillstreet Art Center

Artists of all ages and skill levels converge at **Lillstreet Art Center**, a community hub that got its start in 1975 in a converted horse barn. The current space – a one-time gear factory – hosts adult workshops and classes in seven disciplines, including metal-smithing and jewelry as well as photography, glass-work, and printmaking. In the event you're more of a traditionalist, however, note that ceramics, drawing, and painting are taught here as well. Even first-timers can feel at ease with a special 101 series that inspires fledgling quilters, letter-pressers, and sewers. Meanwhile, kiddos can get creative in the studio with non-competitive camps and classes – clay for toddlers, cartooning for tweens – as well as family workshops that pave the way for side-by-side, generational interaction.

While you're here, take time to explore the gallery, which showcases the work of artists-in-residence, exhibitions, and creations made in its workshops. An on-site store – a treasure trove of souvenirs – is filled with funky, original paintings and drawings, plus handmade, one-of-a-kind accessories and avant-garde ceramics. Unearth dishes to hold trinkets, coffee mugs, or vases.

Then, rub elbows with fellow creatives at the in-house, non-profit **First Slice Pie Café**, a tasty and philanthropic venture where l'Ecole des Arts Culinaires-trained Chef Mary Ellen Diaz serves seasonal, organic fare in quick-serve fashion. That translates to Italian-style chopped salads swathed in red wine vinaigrette; spinach-squash lasagna with mushroom-roasted red pepper dip; and, naturally, some of its namesake: pie.

Lillstreet Art Center; 4401 N. Ravenswood Avenue; tel: 773-769-4226; www.lillstreet.com; various dates and times; charge; map B4

Watch a **Cubs baseball game** – with a better view – from the fringing rooftops

Catching a game at hallowed, ivy-covered **Wrigley Field** may seem like a quintessential experience, but many in the know gripe about inferior sightlines, sub-par food and cramped seating. However, there is an alternative for those wanting to see the Cubs in action: posh rooftop experiences – often multi-level – which hover above the field and, in some cases, fringe the park from neighborhood brownstones. Several sell tickets to individuals, complete with value-added perks. These may include all-inclusive eating and drinking, unobstructed views of the baseball field, or three-course meals paired with local beers. Environs vary from family-friendly to lounge-like. Some spots have shaded bleachers, while others tout floor-to-ceiling windows framing the action on the field. Rooftop venues afford a skybox-like experience, so it's no wonder many offer spacious outdoor patios to revel in the sun.

Post-game, celebrate a win or commiserate with frowning fans – commonplace since the team lost the 1945 World Series – at **Murphy's Bleachers**. This no-frills sports bar, which resides across from the park's bleachers section at Sheffield and Waveland Avenues, is favored by diehards and often packed to the gills. Tired of waiting for a seat? Make your way to **Vines on Clark**. It has great al fresco seating, along with an eclectic, better-than-average menu and budget-friendly drink specials.

Wrigley Field rooftops; see www. wrigleyrooftops.com; www. thewrigleyvillerooftops.com; www. skyboxonsheffield.com; charge; map C3
Murphy's Bleachers; 3655 N. Sheffield Avenue; tel: 773-281-5356; www.murphys bleachers.com; hours vary by season but generally 10am–2am; map C3
Vines on Clark; 3554 N. Clark Street; tel: 773-327-8572; vineswrigley.com; Sun–Fri 11am–2am, Sat 11am–3am; map C2

29

Find **local fashions** at Chicago-centric **Cerato**

Named for a flower thought to promote self-reliance, **Cerato** is a quaint Lakeview boutique brimming with wares from local designers. Swathed in bold, leafy blue wallpaper with warm wood floors and a pressed tin ceiling, the exposed brick storefront houses a carefully edited collection of clothing and accessories. Consider it a go-to for colorful, high-waisted skirts from Kate Boggiano, dresses from Anna Fong and Avery Layne's mod-meets-retro '80s getups, named for fashion icons and worthy of the covetous stares they receive.

The selection of accessories, too, is a sight for sore eyes. Look for everything from statement-making pieces by Juxtapose Jewelry – they're made from re-imagined estate sale finds – to Eastern Indian-influenced chandelier earrings and necklaces from Paoo. Flipping through racks, you may also uncover eco-conscious garments from the label Frei, sewn locally by workers who are fairly compensated. Honed from sustainable materials like bamboo and hemp, the line is the brainchild of Art Institute of Chicago grad Annie Novotny, who employs vegetable-based dyes and recycled details, including tags crafted from spent office paper. Rounding things out, effortlessly fashionable, non-Chicago-based labels – including apparel from Ali Ro – are added into the mix. Call ahead to learn about meet and greets with designers, custom-styling sessions, and gifts-with-purchase specials, aimed at promoting local designers. Events, such as trunk shows and fashion shows, take place regularly, too.

Cerato; 3451 N. Southport Avenue; tel: 773-248-8604; ceratoboutique.com; Mon-Fri 10am-7pm, Sat 10am-6pm, Sun 11am-5pm; map C2

Down some beer and see flicks at the **Brew & View**

Brew & View – an off-nights flipside of concert hall **The Vic** – isn't a place where you actually *watch* a movie. Instead, it's a lively destination where cheap drinks flow freely from three bars, and the latter-run, cult fave or random, B-list-forgettable films take a backseat to fun. The circa 1912 setting – a dramatic vaudeville house with an Italian marble staircase and intricate architectural details – transforms into a boisterous, booze-bathed bash, with crazy-cheap beverage specials – perhaps $4 Long Island iced teas or 75-cent domestic drafts – a major lure for the 21-and-over crowd (those aged 18–21 can carouse sans drinks).

As for food, look to super-salty (though notoriously unavailable) popcorn, candy, and pizza that get the job done. Then again, you can – and probably should – make like a local by having food delivered from area restaurants. This is acceptable, but other 'outside' food is not permitted.

In the spirit of full disclosure, the sound isn't great here, and neither is the eponymous 'view.' However, the silliness of what's on screen – not to mention the convivial vibe that gets rowdier as the night wears on – make this a really fun night out. Adding further appeal, comedians sometimes take the stage after midnight showings on weekends.

The Vic; 3145 N. Sheffield Avenue; tel: 773-929-6713; www.brewview.com; various nights and times; charge; map C2

THE MUSIC BOX THEATRE

If you'd rather actually experience what's showing on-screen, head instead to indie and foreign film-leaning **Music Box Theatre** (3733 N. Southport Avenue; tel: 773-871-6604; www.musicboxtheatre.com; daily at various times; charge; map C3), a moody, throwback palace with a twinkling, cove-lit ceiling, organ chambers, and a vaguely Italian palazzo feel. It's rumored to be haunted by 'Whitey,' a former manager who sleeps forevermore in the lobby.

Fortify on dishes at **Pho 777**, then admire **Prairie-style architecture**

Set amid a sea of Vietnamese places along Uptown's Argyle strip, **Pho 777**, an easy-to-overlook noodle shop, has a secret weapon that draws diners in: amazing, texturally triumphant beef salad. Loaded with mint, sprinkled with peanuts and saturated with enough lime to 'cook' the pink ribbons of meat, it's finished with airy rice crackers that crackle and pop. Although the dining room is nothing to write home about, there's nary a gripe when aromatic, steaming bowls of pho arrive tableside. Get yours filled with flank, brisket, tripe, meatballs, or any combination therein. Then get ready to make it your own, splashing in sauces: hoisin, Sriracha, fish, and soy. Spice it up with a few peppers, and brighten the brew by tossing in hand-torn herbs. Other solid choices range from soul-satisfying hot pots to a nest of pan-fried beef and shrimp noodles, set atop a pool of sweet-savory gravy.

Because the restaurant is rarely crowded and opens early, there's never a bad time to dine. However, there's something particularly sublime about coming here first thing and starting your day with the bracing beef salad. After your meal, wander the neighboring blocks, popping into quaint grocers for fresh southeast Asian produce and condiments. Continue through the Uptown neighborhood, meandering over to Hutchinson Street from Marine Drive, west to Hazel Street. There, you'll find the city's largest concentration of **Prairie-style homes** and mansions, many designed by architect George W. Maher, William Drummond, and Richard E. Schmidt. Over the years, the area has attracted prominent residents, among them Governor James Thompson.

Pho 777; 1065 W. Argyle Street; tel: 773-561-9909; Mon–Fri 9.30am–10pm, Sat–Sun 9am–10pm; map C5

Meet your inner geek – and design your own 'friends' – at **RobotCity Workshop**

Calling all nerds: the **RobotCity Workshop** in Lakeview is a fantasyland for toy and science enthusiasts. Shelves are bursting with robotic buddies of all sizes and colors, t-shirts, and both easy and mind-boggling do-it-yourself kits. Bins with mechanical, electronic, and motor-based parts encourage creativity. Meanwhile, household helpers – including everyone's favorite, the Roomba – are supported by movies and books that follow the theme.

Perhaps most exciting of all, though, are the store's actual workshops, which provide a haven for the sci-fi-minded. Whether you're looking for something practical or wacky, though, this North Sider has a clear mission: to provide an engaging and safe learning environment for the young and young at heart. Offered regularly, classes require participants to purchase a kit of their choosing. Most can be built in about two hours, but those looking to construct more complex creations can expect to attend two sessions. Want to pass off the tots while you enjoy some sightseeing? Half- and-full-day summer camps are an option, too. As an added boon, a huge catalog of parts,

kits, and gifts can also be ordered online, meaning there's plenty of fun to be had wherever you are. The store also offers a soldering class for enthusiasts age 13-plus.

Since a visit will leave you in a playful state of mind, end the day at nearby **Uncle Fun**, a bonanza of shenanigans – be it gag gifts, peculiar books, fun figurines, or useless (though endlessly entertaining) odds and ends.

Robot City Workshop; 3226 N. Sheffield Avenue; tel: 773-281-1008; robotcityworkshop.com; daily 11am–7pm; map C2
Uncle Fun; 1338 W. Belmont Avenue; tel: 773-477-8223; www.unclefunchicago. com; Mon–Fri noon–7pm, Sat 11am–7pm, Sun 11am–5pm; map C2

Scare yourself silly at historic **Graceland Cemetery**

Constructed during the Victorian era, historic, pastoral **Graceland Cemetery** in Uptown is as creepy as it is cool. Filled with notable tombs and headstones – including the grave of, and a mausoleum built by, architect Louis Sullivan – this 19th-century, park-like plot is a tranquil, self-professed oasis of horticulture, art, and architecture, albeit one that is said to be stalked by ghosts. The grounds are open to all, and individual or group tours can be arranged through the **Chicago History Museum** *(p.81)*. Self-guided tours also prove popular; you'd be wise to stop by the office and purchase a copy of the **Chicago Architecture Foundation**'s *A Walk Through Graceland Cemetery*, by Barbara Lanctot. With this in hand, wander

the immaculately maintained grounds. You may come across memorials to world heavyweight Jack Johnson, baseball's William Hulbert, and Charles Wacker of Wacker Drive fame. You'll also encounter the final resting places of industrialists and merchants from George Pullman to Phillip Armour, a meatpacking baron. Other notable architect residents include John Root, Daniel Burnham, Ludwig Mies van der Rohe, and Fazlur Khan, designer of the Willis Tower downtown.

While you're here, be sure to see the historic Arts and Craft-style chapel. Constructed of Midwestern-quarried red granite, it has seen expansions and, recently, a restoration. Now, it houses end-of-life accommodations in the form of in-ground burials, garden columbarium walls, and hundreds of hand-carved niches to hold cremated remains. While you're here, you can also commune with eternal residents beneath old-growth trees amid native plants.

Graceland Cemetery; 4001 N. Clark Street; tel: 773-525-1105; www.graceland cemetery.org; entrance free, self-guided tours with $5 map; Chicago Architecture Foundation tours charge for non-members; Sun 2pm Aug–Oct; map C4

Troll through **tinctures and toiletries** at holistic **Merz Apothecary**

Located in Lincoln Square, a neighborhood known for its Old-World charm and German heritage, **Merz Apothecary** dates back to 1875. The brainchild of Swiss pharmacist Peter Merz, it has stood the test of time. Granted, it has changed hands and moved from its original Lakeview digs, but it continues to exude turn-of-the-19th-century pharmacy appeal, complete with wood-trimmed and leaded-glass details. Homeopathic and herbal medicines are an undeniable draw, but there's another more tempting reason to stop by: it's a product junkie's dream. Chock-full of some 600 brands, it tempts with Vetiver & Rum shave cream, scents from L'Artisan Parfumeur,

and chemical and toxin-free deodorant roll-ons and powders from Duggan Sisters. It's also a go-to for Diptyque candles, essential oils, and room sprays as well as licorice, pastilles, and candies from afar.

Having shopped until your carry-on will burst, sign up for its bath of the month club; available in three-, six- or 12-month increments; it ensures indulgences arrive at your door long after the flight back home. And to carry on the girlie fun, ladies can go on and get a 'vintage' coif at **Tigerlilie Salon**, a funky beauty parlor specializing in up-dos from the 1940s through 1970s as well as bobs, pixie cuts, and piled-high bouffants. Sweetening the pot, the shop also carries its own line of hair accessories – great take-homes for a special gal. Also of note, the shop hosts monthly pinup sessions, complete with a photographer.

Merz Apothecary; 4716 N. Lincoln Avenue; tel: 773-989-0900; www.small flower.com; Mon-Sat 9am-6pm; map A5
Tigerlilie Salon; 4755 N. Lincoln Avenue; tel: 773-506-7870; www. tigerlilie.com; Tue-Fri 11am-8pm, Sat 10am-6pm; map A5

BYOB (and bring cash) to **Chilam Balam**, Chuy Valencia's sustainable **Mexican small plates** stunner

Plan ahead and bring your own hooch to **Chilam Balam,** a hyped – but hidden-feeling – cash-only Mexican in Lakeview. If you bring spirits, you'll want to mix what you procure with limeade or virgin sangria, house mixers that result in BYO imbibing made just to your taste.

The restaurant shares a name with the handwritten, mostly 18th century, Yucatec collection of Mayan miscellanies, which range topically from mysticism to medical and are attributed to a prophetic priest, Chilam Balam. There's no hocus pocus to food preparations, though – just young Chuy Valencia, who turns out wildly flavorful, beyond-colorful farm-to-table cuisine that's both precise and playful in its execution, all served in a brightly hued, artifact-adorned subterranean setting.

Growing up in Sonoma, California, Valencia's parents cultivated food in the backyard; his grandfather also grew fruit and vegetables and raised livestock in his parents' hometown of Colima, Mexico. All ingrained in him the importance of using quality ingredients as well as a reverence of where food comes from, facts that clearly shine in his product-driven plates. Having spent time in the kitchens of Rick Bayless' Topolobampo and Frontera Grill as well as Adobo Grill, Valencia went about creating a eco-minded gathering place that is as perfect for casual dates as it is nights out with friends. Its regularly changing, seasonally inspired dishes are made for sharing – though the truth is you may wind up gobbling them down solo. In other words, feel free to order two; this sophisticated cuisine, thankfully, comes at an affordable price point.

One visit may yield crispy veal sweetbreads with Pueblan *tinga*, house-made chorizo, avocado, and *queso fresco*; another may mean suckling pig, accented by *verdolagas* and *cascabel*-tomato sauce, and served with hushpuppies. If you have more of a sweet tooth, try the roasted duck breast with hazelnut sauce, smoked cacao nibs, a toasted ancho marshmallow, and cookie crumbs. Traditionalists will appreciate the fact that they can get the classics, too: chunky guacamole, *flautas* stuffed with chicken thigh, and lime-blasted blue marlin *ceviche* dotted with habanero, cucumbers, and

tomatoes. Naturally, desserts
– be it hibiscus flan or peanut
butter-filled *empanadas* with fruit
compote – are no less enticing.
Wash finales down with Oaxacan
hot chocolate.

In the event you can't procure
a table, there are many other
fab Mexican meals to be had
around town – especially in the
city's culturally rich Pilsen
neighborhood. However, if
it's a BYO bent you seek,
consider staying close to
where you are, choosing
to dine at any number of
eclectic spots. Among
the appealing options are
New Mexican **Abiquiu
Café** (1034 W. Belmont
Avenue; tel: 773-577-
3917; map C2), Peruvian
Machu Picchu for lomo
saltado (3856 N. Ashland
Avenue; tel: 773-472-0471;
map B3), and Neapolitan
Sapore di Napoli, an
always hopping pie hole
and gelateria (1406 W.
Belmont Avenue; tel:
773-935-1212; map C2).

*Chilam Balam; 3023 N. Broadway
Street; tel: 773-296-6901; www.chilam
balamchicago.com; Tue–Thur 5-10pm,
Fri–Sat 5-11pm; map D1*

After some liquid courage, sing (with friends) at
Lincoln Karaoke

It'd be easy to overlook **Lincoln Karaoke**, a nondescript – even shady-looking – spot in Lincoln Square. But if you have a thing for singing, you'll want to check it out. Appealing to a diverse collective – shy guys, partiers, and those who simply appreciate a bit of personal space – this affordable late-night haunt features a labyrinth of private rooms equipped with flat-panel TVs, light-up tambourines, and cushy sofas, not to mention a thousands-strong catalog of popular American, Chinese, and Korean tunes. Select them using an oversize, novelty remote control, wait for the light show to kick in, and belt out your favorite tunes with the best (and worst) of them.

Given the availability of potent, candy-colored libations, cheekily named shots, and free-flowing beers – rounds of which can easily send you to the moon – it's fortunate to know a menu is on hand to ward off hangovers. Work your way through sets of your favorite tunes while snapping up Asian wings, kalbi, or kimchi fried rice. Or consider slurping up a bowl of ramen.

Be mindful that the place gets busy on weekends, making reservations a pre-requisite. Should you show up on a whim and find all rooms accounted for, head to **Hidden Cove Lounge**, a raucous dive bar down the road where, starting at 8pm nightly, karaoke is king and drinks are rock-bottom cheap. Depending on the night, you might also catch a dart or national trivia competition in action.

Lincoln Karaoke; 5526 N. Lincoln Avenue; tel: 773-895-2299; www.lincolnkaraoke.com; Sun-Fri 7pm-2am, Sat 7pm-3am; charge; map A6
Hidden Cove Lounge; 5336 N. Lincoln Avenue; tel: 773-275-6711; nightly 2pm-4am; charge; map A6

Walk among the flowers and tranquil fountains at rambling **Gethsemane Garden Center**

Urban landscapes aren't exactly known for tranquility. That's where a place like Andersonville's rambling, blocks-long **Gethsemane Garden Center** comes in. In winter, wander through its sultry greenhouse – filled with bonsai, succulents, cacti, and lush, towering tropical plants – and feel transported. Come summer, revel in its vast selection of annuals and perennials, including a large array of hellebores. Take in the array of fruiting plants and vegetables, too, from Red Sails lettuce and Bolivian Rainbow peppers to elderberry bushes, Crimson Red rhubarb, and Riesentraube tomatoes.

The gift-giving possibilities are bountiful, too, since hand-made necklaces from local artisans, floral coasters, and hand-painted Bavarian pewter are on hand. Every bit as impressive is the collection of rough-hewn pots tucked into nooks, cast-stone birdbaths, and trickling fountains. The store also stocks plenty of patio furniture, outdoor accessories, and centrepiece-worthy Weber Grills for those who can take them home.

While you're here, walk among the trees and shrubs, and – should the timing be right – attend an informative workshop or lecture, as they're hosted periodically throughout the year. Whatever you do, don't be afraid to ask questions of its knowledgeable, friendly horticulturalists – or to visit during an 'off' season. Sales and year-round décor make visits worthwhile whatever the weather.

Gethsemane Garden Center; 5739 N. Clark Street; tel: 773-878-5915; www. gethsemanegardens.com; call for seasonal hours ; map B7

39

Eat grub grown on the rooftop while catching a show at eco-conscious **Uncommon Ground**

There's much ado about the 2,500-sq-ft (232-sq-m), certified organic rooftop garden at **Uncommon Ground,** a beloved Wrigleyville venue. Hovering above residential buildings are a rotating, diverse array of crops, including heirloom tomatoes, fennel, and bush beans, along with fragrant, thriving herbs and plantings derived from the slow food movement's Ark of Taste. The yield – supplemented by what's grown and produced at like-minded, local farms – is used at the on-site restaurant's menu. The end result is dishes like crispy potato ravioli with caramelized cauliflower puree,

pickled cauliflower, and capers; house-smoked Polish sausage with German potato salad; and a knock-your-socks-off, grown-up grilled cheese tucked with Honeycrisp apples, caramelized onions, mushrooms, and mustard.

During the summer, tours of the rooftop can be arranged in advance for a nominal fee, and a first Friday farmers' market is held evenings on site from June through September. Of course, whether it's the growing season or not, there's plenty to love inside the restaurant – from the rustic dining room with flickering fireplaces to the open mic nights, live musical performances, and house-infused spirits that warm one from the inside out. (Be sure to try the vegetable take on a bloody Mary, built from stout and smoked poblano, onion, roasted bell pepper, and garlic-infused vodka, and finished with a vegetable skewer.) Also watch for free, environmentally focused 'green room sessions,' held each month to benefit a rare fruit orchard initiative.

Uncommon Ground; 1401 W. Devon Avenue; tel: 773-465-9801; www. uncommonground.com; Sun-Thur 9am-midnight; Fri-Sat 9am-2am; map C8

Take a tour and **taste tipples** at the boutique
Koval Distillery

Prohibition left an indelible mark on Chicago's history, and bootlegger Al Capone was the underbelly's face. Nowadays, cocktail culture is celebrated and pre-Prohibition-era and speakeasy libations are a virtual way of life. Nowhere is this more evident than at **Koval Distillery** in Ravenswood. It's a labor of love for ex-academic husband and wife team Robert and Sonat Birnecker, who employ the techniques of his Austrian grandfather, a distiller, to turn out spirits that are both organic and kosher. Come to its store and tasting room, and prepare to choose between white whiskey made from Midwest wheat; pear brandy; and clear, smooth vodka distilled from rye. Accordingly, cocktail-ready chrysanthemum-honey, orange blossom, and rose hip liqueurs vie for attention, along with unfiltered, single-barrel Lion's Pride whiskey, which comes in millet, spelt, wheat, oat, and rye varieties. Plan ahead and attend a two-hour whiskey workshop, which trains taste buds and reveals the history of bourbon and whiskey in America, the difference between classic and modern distillation techniques, and – in libation-speak – what heads, hearts, and tails really are.

You can also sample Koval's wares at bars and restaurants around town, including at **The Bad Apple** (4300 N. Lincoln Avenue; tel: 773-360-8406; map A4), **Big Jones** (5347 N. Clark Street; tel: 773-275-5725; map B6), and **Frontier** (1072 N. Milwaukee Avenue; tel: 773-772-4322; map p107 G2). \

Chicago's past is beer-saturated as well – look to the Lager Beer Riot of 1855 for proof of that. Places like **Goose Island Beer Company** (1800 N. Clybourn Avenue; tel: 312-915-0071; map p.44 C2) and **Half Acre Beer Company** (4257 N. Lincoln Avenue; tel: 773-248-4038; map p.24 A4) keep this spirit alive.

Koval Distillery; 5121 N. Ravenswood Avenue; tel: 312-878-7988; www.koval-distillery.com; store: Mon–Fri 1–6pm; charge for tours and workshops; map B5

Lincoln Park and Old Town

| 0 | 200 | 400 | 600 | 800 | 1000 yds |
| 0 | 200 | 400 | 600 | 800 | 1000 m |

Alfred Caldwell Lily Pond **E4**
Alinea **D2**
Apollo Theatre **C4**
The Belden Stratford Hotel **E4**
Café Brauer **E3**
CB2 **D2**
Charlie Trotter's **D3**
Chicago History Museum **F2**
Crate & Barrel **C2**
Crate & Barrel Outlet **C2**
Delilah's **C5**
Diversey Driving Range **E5**
Diversey Miniature Golf **E5**
Floating World Gallery **C3**
Fullerton Avenue Beach **F4**
The House of Glunz **E1**
Goose Island Beer
  Company **C2**
Green City Market **F2**
Isabella Fine Lingerie **C3**
Jayson Home and Garden **C3**
Liars Club **A4**
Lincoln Hall **C4**
Lincoln Park Conservatory **E4**
Lincoln Park Zoo **E4**
North Avenue Beach **G3**

North Pond **E5**
Old Town Aquarium **E2**
Old Town Oil **E2**
Old Town School of Folk
  Music **C3**
Old Town Social **E2**
Park West **E3**
Peggy Notebaert Nature
  Museum **E4**
Rotofugi Designer Toy Store
  & Gallery **B5**
The Royal George **D2**
St Michael **E2**
The Second City Training
  Center **E2**
The Spice House **E2**
Stanley's Kitchen & Tap **E3**
Steppenwolf Theatre **D2**
Theater on the Lake **F4**
Trotter's To Go **B4**
Victory Gardens
  Biograph Theater **C4**
Village Cycle Center **E1**
Zanies Comedy Club **E2**

Rub elbows with **Chicago chefs** at **Green City Market**, then explore the **Peggy Notebaert Nature Museum**

Operating outdoors from May-October at the south end of Lincoln Park or indoors at **Peggy Notebaert Nature Museum**, **Green City Market** is where chefs – and produce-conscious Chicagoans – mingle. Wander the stalls, and chat with local farmers, who sell rainbow-hued fruits and vegetables, meat from responsibly raised animals, and cheeses from local farmsteads. It's also a great place to find fresh-cut flowers, midwestern maple syrup, fresh-baked bread, and confections, such as *pate de fruit*. Be sure to come hungry since there are plenty of prepared foods, too, from doughnuts to tamales. Plan to spend some time here in summer: workshops on edible gardens, cooking demonstrations from top chefs and food-loving festivals are ways to engage. And if you can, plan to attend its popular Chef's Barbecue Benefit, held each July and brimming with food from more than 100 restaurants.

While you're here, make friends with butterflies at the Notebaert's indoor haven, where 75

OLD TOWN FOODIE STOPS
Notable nibbles – from olive oils to aged balsamic vinegars – are plentiful in these parts. Find standouts at **Old Town Oil** (1520 N. Wells Street; tel: 312-787-9595), where spigotted, stainless steel fustis of extra-virgin olive oil and vinegar are bottled and sealed on the spot. At aromatic **The Spice House** (1512 N. Wells Street; tel: 312-274-0378), uncover the appeal of Lake Shore Drive, a seasoning blend made for mixing in omelets, sprinkling atop corn-on-the-cob, and showering on fish. If you merely want a snack – and a serious one at that – pop into the on-site butcher shop at **Old Town Social** (455 W. North Avenue; tel: 312-266-2277), where you can customize a charcuterie basket. Odds are, you'll be just as happy if you load up on fennel-laced finocchiona, smoky chorizo, and pepperoni padded with dehydrated red bell peppers. Whether you choose peppery summer sausage or spicy soppressata, there's something that'll make your hotel room smell sublime – while it lasts.

---

exotic species flutter freely from tree-to-tree. You can also learn about birds that are native to Illinois, engage in water play at the River Works exhibit and get educated about endangered wetland species. Time it right to see water snakes and praying mantises get fed. Or walk any time through re-creations of different environments, from prairies to savannahs.

Then, if weather allows, take respite at the **Alfred Caldwell Lily Pool**, located south of Fullerton Avenue in Lincoln Park. Its history dates back to 1889, when it was built for raising tropical water lilies. Redesigned in the Prairie style in the 1930s by Alfred Caldwell, it's meant to mimic a glacial flow cutting through limestone. Near its north end, a waterfall represents the source of the 'river.' A reflective sanctuary for visitors, it's filled with wildlife and fringed with thousands of native prairie and woodland wildflowers. Its hidden location is a real plus – many a resident has overlooked it on a morning run.

Green City Market; Clark Street and Lincoln Avenue; tel: 773-880-1266; free; map F2

Peggy Notebaert Nature Museum; 2430 N. Cannon Drive; tel: 773-755-5100; www.naturemuseum.org; Mon–Fri 9am-4.30pm, Sat–Sun 10am-5pm; charge; map E4

Alfred Caldwell Lily Pool; Fullerton Avenue at Cannon Drive; tel: 312-742-7529; www.chicagoparkdistrict.com; free; map E4

Get the last laugh, while taking a **sketch comedy or writing class**, at **The Second City Training Center**

Comedy and Chicago go hand in hand, thanks to **The Second City** in Old Town. At one time a University of Chicago-born cabaret revue, its first production debuted in 1959. By 1961, it sent a cast to Broadway with a Tony nomination intact. From there, it grew beyond a single stage to become a bastion for improv, one that's served as a training ground for celeb comics Stephen Colbert, Mike Myers, Steve Carell, and Tina Fey; this school of comedy has been exporting talents to *Saturday Night Live* since the 1970s. Featuring multiple touring companies, it hosts training

centers in Chicago, Toronto, and Los Angeles. Locally, **The Second City Training Center** ushers fledgling jokesters into sketch and improv comedy with classes in the performance arts for all skill levels.

Whether it's instruction in standup you seek, hope to become a director, or would like to learn the art of voiceover, they're covered here. So too, are the genres of comedic songwriting, rap, body movement, and improv- and comedy-writing. If you're only in town for a few days, sign up for its three-day intensive program, which covers the bases at a rapid-fire rate. Those with a bit more time should consider a week-long immersion, which offers an intensive improvisational experience. Then again, you could always just swing by **Zanies Comedy Club** for laughs. After all, it was the stomping ground of luminaries such as Jay Leno, Jerry Seinfeld, Tim Allen, and Roseanne Barr.

The Second City Training Center; 1608 N. Wells Street; tel: 312-664-3959; www.secondcity.com/training; charge; map E2
Zanies Comedy Club; 1548 N. Wells Street; tel: 312-337-4027; www.chicago. zanies.com; charge; map E2

Meander over to **Lincoln Park Zoo**, home to **1,200 animals** – backdropped by skyscrapers

Perched in the heart of the city, adjacent to the scenic paths of Lake Michigan and Lincoln Park proper, this gratis sanctuary resides in the shadows of Chicago's looming, architectural skyline. At any time of day, **Lincoln Park Zoo** may reverberate with lions' roars or showcase polar bears romping and swimming in a habitat with underwater viewing. The soaring trees and landscaped grounds are one thing, the dry-thorn or verdant tropical rainforests and savannas another. Take a walk through the Pritzker Family Children's Zoo, home to red wolves and North American river otters; see primates of all persuasions; and revel in the beauty of the swans and waterfowl pool. Take time to converse with the apes, who lounge and frolic in bamboo and strangler fig forests, or 'journey' to Africa to see Eastern black rhinoceroses, cichlids of several kinds, and massive, grey-skinned pygmy hippopotamuses.

When you're ready to take a load off, visit the carousel – it features carved, ride-on wooden animals. Or hop aboard the zoo's train ride. Continue your day with on-site bites at the seasonal, picturesque **Café Brauer** or organic **Café at Wild Things**. The zoo houses a handful of shops, too, and they're filled with hand-crafted gifts and jewelry. Be sure to watch for special events that take place on the grounds throughout the year. Among the most popular is holiday-lit **Zoo Lights**, when Santa's safari makes an appearance and ice carving demonstrations take place. Beyond that, festivities may include garden tours and parties, family campouts and picnics as well as yoga classes, talks and workshops for all ages.

Lincoln Park Zoo; 2001 N. Clark Street; tel: 312-742-2000; www.lpzoo.org; daily Nov–Mar 10am-4.30pm, Apr–May and Sept–Oct 10am-5pm, May 29–Sept 6 Mon–Fri 10am-5pm, Sat–Sun 10am-6.30pm; free; map E4

Go for broke and dine at **Charlie Trotter's** or **Alinea**

Chicago is a food-lover's city, being home to countless renowned chefs, including Charlie Trotter, whose namesake restaurant, **Charlie Trotter's**, helped position Chicago as a culinary hotspot. He and his protégés continue to create some of the most intricate plates in town, serving them in a sedate Lincoln Park brownstone in spendy, set-price fashion. The multi-plate affair is ever-changing, but may include dishes such as 48-hour braised veal breast with curried eggplant, arugula, and wild capers. When you're really feeling flush, book the kitchen table, which boasts its own luxurious (and even more stratospherically priced) menu.

Close by, Grant Achatz takes a different, jaw-dropping approach at **Alinea**, where dishes defy classification and often require instruction to (properly) consume. Throughout, wild flavor pairings – perhaps halibut with black pepper, coffee, and lemon – ensure there's plenty to discuss for the duration of the lengthy, prix-fixe experience.

As not everyone can buffer such splurges, it's good to know both chefs offer budget-friendly alternatives. Trotter has a grab-and-go, prepared food store, **Trotter's To Go** (1337 W. Fullerton Avenue; tel: 773-868-6510; map B4), while Achatz, on the other hand, mans by-ticket-only dining destination **Next** (953 W. Fulton Market; tel: 312-226-0858; map p.86 A5) in the West Loop. But since dining there requires planning far in advance, his adjacent, no-reservations-required **Aviary** (955 W. Fulton Market; www.theaviary. com; map p.86 A5) – a conceptual cocktail lounge with chic nibbles – may be a better bet.

Charlie Trotter's; 816 W. Armitage Avenue; tel: 773-248-6228; www. charlietrotters.com; Tue–Fri 6–9pm, Sat 5.30–6.15pm or 8.30-9.15pm; map D3 Alinea; 1723 N. Halsted Street; tel: 312-867-0110; www.alinea-restaurant.com; Wed–Sun 5-9.30pm; map D2

Marvel at the exotic aquatic life at **Old Town Aquarium**, then discover Japanese art at **Floating World Gallery**

Fin fanatics converge at **Old Town Aquarium,** a longtime shop that designs and installs fresh and saltwater aquariums. A nautical – and soothing – vibe permeates the place, its stunning selection of fish procured by Jim Walters and Ian Schakowsky, who dive to the deepest reaches to find rare, colorful marine life, which boasts a variety among the largest in the country. Its fish originate the world over, from Bali to Brazil, the Solomon Islands to Jakarta. You'll see regal angels flitting between rocks, a rainbow's-worth of starfish, and showy, turquoise-hued broomtail wrasse. Strange, striped catfish, shiny, humphead glassfish, and thriving underwater plants further the theme. The freshwater fish and plants are interesting, too, especially the gliding stingrays. Those looking to buy should turn to the helpful, veteran staff, who are at the ready to fashion sustainable aquatic environments that make sense.

While you're in the area, continue on to explore local galleries, perhaps **Floating World Gallery**, an impressive destination for Japanese contemporary art. Named for 'ukiyo-e' – images of a fading, beautiful world – it's a favorite among private collectors, who come to its auctions in search of both modern woodblocks and wondrous paintings. It's also a place with an educational bent; seminars shed light on history and techniques or allow peeks at works normally behind glass. From there, continue to other art galleries in the **Old Town Triangle** (www. oldtowntriangle.com).

Old Town Aquarium; 1538 N. Wells Street; tel: 312-642-8763; www. oldtownaquarium.com; Mon-Fri noon-7pm, Tue and Thur until 8pm, Sat 11am-6pm, Sun noon-6pm; map E2 Floating World Gallery; 1925 N. Halsted Street; tel: 312-587-7800; www. floatingworld.com; Tue-Fri 1-5pm and by appointment; map C3

Get inspired by the modern and vintage furniture collection at **Jayson Home and Garden**

Located in a converted warehouse in Lincoln Park, earthy, eclectic, and ever-changing **Jayson Home and Garden** showcases a singular collection of upholstered and vintage French and Asian pieces. Its unique flea market finds – such as vintage canisters, antiqued hand mirrors, modern and statement-making brass lamps – save patrons the trouble of traveling the globe. There's also a unique collection of window boxes and modern, cylindrical, and angular pots – including ones already filled with flowers. Its urban garden is a Zen oasis of orchids and jades as well as trees and herbs, and it offers a container planting service perfect for those who love gardening but lack vision.

The shop is also known for its fine floral arrangements, be it *echeveria* in a gold ceramic box or a simple grouping of ruby and yellow calla lilies. After entertaining a bouquet buy, contemplate an investment in natural horn cups, faux zebra pillows, and mercury glass votives; sniff out Miller Harris candles; or buy a funky-cool, framed linoleum print as a gift to yourself.

After you've found inspiration, walk the corridor of North and Clybourn Avenues to find other specialty furniture stores, including the flagship **CB2** (800 W. North Ave; tel: 312-787-8329; map D2), the modern offshoot of **Crate & Barrel** (850 W. North Avenue; tel: 312-573-9800; map C2), the American home retailer that got its start in Old Town in 1962. Nearby, you'll also find the **Crate & Barrel Outlet** (1864 N. Clybourn Avenue; tel: 312-787-4775; map C2). Fashion lovers may also want to go on a spree at the **Wells Street boutiques**.

Jayson Home and Garden; 1885 N. Clybourn Avenue; tel: 800-472-1885; www.jaysonhomeandgarden.com; Mon and Thur 9am–8pm, Tue, Wed and Fri 9am–6pm, Sat 10am–5pm, Sun 11am–5pm; map C3

Down whiskeys at divey Delilah's, or nurse your hangover at a bloody Mary bar

Delilah's is a punky Lincoln Park bar, located near Lincoln, Diversey, and Racine, and it's legendary among Chicagoans despite its seedy exterior and dingy, bi-level environs. But never fear, by taking a leap of faith, you'll be met with a 500-plus selection of bottled whiskey, walls hung with local art and music curated by some of the city's best DJs. Located in a former speakeasy that dates back to 1909, the bar is open 365 days a year, and it hosts an ongoing roster of events, including tastings, free movies, and themed music nights that celebrate luminaries like Sid Vicious and Morrissey. Much of the appeal of the place can be attributed to its diverse, come-as-you-are vibe, a fact that's reflected in the music you'll hear. One

night may usher in skater faves, while rockabilly is showcased on another. Nightly drink specials and free pool on Mondays further fuel the fun. Accordingly, games like Donkey Kong and pinball make the hours fly by.

Since over-imbibing is likely, plan a morning-after trip to **Stanley's Kitchen & Tap**, which hosts an all-you-can-eat fried chicken brunch and bloody Mary bar. Even non-drinkers can take comfort in the Southern-bent menu. It's brimming with pleasing possibilities, including fried green dill pickles and okra; Tater Tot poutine heaped with applewood bacon, two cheeses, and gravy; and blackened catfish with greens. There's also a large American whiskey selection poured here, in addition to spiked milkshakes, Texas tea, and a regular rotation of shot specials, if a hair of the dog cure is desired.

Delilah's; 2771 N. Lincoln Avenue; tel: 773-472-2771; www.delilahschicago. com; Sun-Fri 4pm-2am, Sat 4pm-3am; map C5
Stanley's Kitchen & Tap; 1970 N. Lincoln Avenue; tel: 312-642-0007; www. stanleyskitchenandtap.com; Mon-Fri 11am-2am, Sat-Sun 10am-2am, brunch offer Sun 10am-4pm; map E3

Have a **theatrical experience** in Lincoln Park

When it comes to theater in town, history runs deep. According to the Encyclopedia of Chicago, the first professional performance took place in 1834. At the cost of 50-cents per adult and a quarter per child, it featured a pyro ventriloquist named Mr. Bowers. It turned out well, traveling showmen proved popular, and the city's first formal venue – the legendary Chicago Theatre, then housed in a vacant dining room of an old hotel – began entertaining audiences. Today, the Loop Theater District is a force to be reckoned with.

So, too, is the district in **Lincoln Park**, which came into its own in the 1960s and 1970s. It's now the site of prestigious productions at houses like **The Royal George** (1641 N. Halsted Street; tel: 312-988-9000; map D2), **Steppenwolf Theatre** (1650 N. Halsted Street; tel: 312-335-1650; map D2), **Victory Gardens Biograph Theater** (2433 N. Lincoln Avenue; tel: 773-871-3000; map C4), and **Apollo Theater** (2540 N. Lincoln Avenue; tel: 773-935-6100; map C4). In-season, you can also catch a show at **Theater on the Lake** (2401 N. Lake Shore Drive; tel: 312-742-7994; map F4), a Prairie style, waterside building that stages shows from noteworthy Chicago companies.

If plays aren't your thing, there are plenty of other entertainment options near here, from live tunes at **Park West** (322 W. Armitage Avenue; tel: 773-929-1322; map E3) to dancing at rowdy punk rocker **Liar's Club** (1665 W. Fullerton Avenue; tel: 773-665-1110; map A4).

Eye plants at the **Lincoln Park Conservatory**, and eat **organic fare** at North Pond

Built by architect Joseph L. Silsbee between 1890–95 in an effort to propagate (and show off) exotic plants and those grown for use in Chicago parks, the four-season **Lincoln Park Conservatory** has been billed as a 'paradise under glass' since its inception. Lushly tropical and punctuated by rock-fringed ponds filled with aquatic plants, it has four display houses: palm and orchid houses filled with fragile and fanciful things, a fern room, and a show room that hosts picturesque, four-season flower shows. From banana, cacao, and sour sop to air plants, Spanish moss, and prey-trapping carnivorous plants, there's a lot to see. Keep a lookout for the Scheelea palm, acquired by the Field Museum in Brazil in 1929, and the cycads – one of the oldest plant species on Earth. You can take a free, educational tour with a docent during designated hours on Friday, Saturday and Sunday.

After you've immersed yourself in the conservatory's beauty, wander outdoors; surrounding the structure are colorful, outdoor annual gardens. Wander the lovely park at leisure, but be certain to finish the day at Bruce Sherman's Arts and Crafts-style dining room, **North Pond**, where you can tuck into an organic, locally grown meal and hand-crafted, artisanal wines. Originally constructed as a warming house for ice skaters, the place oozes charm and sophistication. So does the menu, which features oft-changing, hyper-seasonal dishes. Consider visiting for the Sunday set-price brunch, when options may include a sunny-side-up egg and vanilla waffle with house-smoked bacon, pecans, and maple-cherry syrup.

Lincoln Park Conservatory; 2391 N. Stockton Drive; tel: 312-742-7736; www.chicagoparkdistrict.com; daily 9am–5pm; free; map E4
North Pond; 2610 N. Cannon Drive; tel: 773-477-5845; www.northpond restaurant.com; Tue–Sat 5.30–9.15pm, Sun 10.30am–1pm, 5.30–8.30pm; map E5

55

Relive your youth – in stylish fashion – at **Rotofugi Designer Toy Store & Gallery**

Whatever your age, the wondrous finds at **Rotofugi Designer Toy Store & Gallery** never cease to impress. Tucked into a vintage flatiron building at the fringe of Lincoln Park and Lakeview, it's the work of husband and wife team Kirby and Whitney Kerr, who stock the shelves with designer whimsy: vinyl and resin figures, plush monsters and capsule toys from creators the world over. Scope out its signature, kooky line of artist-designed figures: there's even a toasted marshmallow man, made in conjunction with Chicago-based Squibbles Ink. From there, it's on to funky cupcake magnets,

pink and yellow horned monsters, and schoolyard justice-seeking characters.

Mind you, it's not *all* about fun and games. Beastly flash drives, Uglydoll totes, and creature-like, portable speakers serve a purpose, too. Adding allure, items are available at all price points, ranging from inexpensive key chains and kitschy ice cube trays to exclusive collectibles. Don't forget to check out the t-shirts and accessories either – glow-in-the-dark garb holds court with playful hats. Around every corner are items that inspire laughs, smack of hip nursery décor, and make you feel like a kid again.

Once you've taken care of business, peruse the shop gallery – it's hung with monthly exhibitions from artists near and far, many of them furthering the modern pop art feel. Openings are usually held from 7–10pm on the first day of an exhibit, may be DJ-backed and usually have artists in attendance. See something you love? The good news is works are for sale.

Rotofugi Designer Toy Store & Gallery; 2780 N. Lincoln Avenue; tel: 773-868-3308; rotofugi.com; daily 11am–7pm; map B5

Succumb to from-the-vines vintages at historic
The House of Glunz

Historic and locally beloved, family-run **The House of Glunz** dates back to 1888. Exuding the charm of another time and place, its tasting room is trimmed with gilt-framed portraits and antique furnishings. Artifacts throughout point to the days when fortified wines arrived from Spain and Portugal in casks and were aged and bottled in its cellar. While you're here, do check out the tavern room, where you'll find fine, artisan-made goblets. Awe-inspiring, too, is its rare wine cellar, which contains luxury potables, such as Hirsch 16 Year Old Reserve straight bourbon whiskey or a bottle of Penfolds Grange 2003 from the Barossa Valley. Separate of that, the large, thoughtful Old and New World wines ring in at every price point, and a range of cordials, sake, and hand-crafted spirits offer palate-pleasing alternatives. It's no wonder oenophiles clamour to attend its wine-themed trips abroad.

The store also stocks a selection of things to go with, from classic and specialty caviars to chocolates, sausages, and condiments. You'll also find barware essentials, such as corkscrews, decanters, and absinthe fountains, glasses, and spoons. Come on Fridays and Saturdays for **complimentary tastings**: they showcase new arrivals. To save cash, look out for end-of-bin and seasonal sales, or attend one of the regularly offered vino classes, hosted at its Old Town digs. Using this as your launching pad, continue on and catch a performance at **River North Dance Company** (1016 N. Dearborn Street; tel: 312-944-2888), or see a concert or take a class at **Old Town School of Folk Music** (909 W. Armitage Avenue; tel: 773-728-6000). Then, as a nightcap, toast with those Glunz bottles you splurged on.

The House of Glunz; 1206 N. Wells Street; tel: 312-642-3000; thehouseof glunz.com; Mon–Fri 10am–8pm, Sat 10am–7pm, Sun 2–5pm; map E1

Gold Coast,
Magnificent Mile,
Streeterville
and River North

0   100 200 300 400 500 yds
0   100 200 300 400 500 m

Ⓐ Clark Street
Ⓜ Chicago History Museum
W. North Ave
East North Boulevard
Ⓑ Archbishop's Residence
Ⓜ International Museum of Surgical Science
Ⓒ
Ⓓ
N

Ⓐ
Ⓑ
W. North Ave
East North Boulevard
North Clark Street
North LaSalle Drive
North Wells Street
N. Weiland St
State P'way
N. Dearborn
Astor Street
N. Lake Shore Drive

Ⓔ W. Burton St
East Burton Place
International Museum of Surgical Science

N. Wells Street
W. Schiller Street
East Schiller Street
East Schiller Street

GOLD COAST
N. LaSalle Drive
North State Street
Former Playboy Mansion
N. Dearborn Street
East Banks Street
Astor Street
Ritchie Court
N. Lake Shore Drive

West Goethe Street
Goethe St
E. Scott Street
N. Stone St

Ⓙ
Red Line
Clark/Division
Chicago Food Planet

West Division St
East Division Street

Chicago Q
Chicago Elm Street
East
Oak Street Beach
Bike and Roll

Ashkenaz
East Cedar Street

Mr. Kite's Confectionery
East Maple Street

W. Hill St
NEAR NORTH
East Bellevue Street

W. Wendell St
East Oak Street
E. Lake Shore Dr.
The Drake Hotel

Ⓒ West Oak Street
Red Line
East Walton Place
East Delaware Place

W. Walton St
WASHINGTON SQUARE
Magnificent Mile
John Hancock Center

W. Locust St
E. Delaware Pl.
Four Seasons 900 Shops
East Chestnut Street

N. Franklin Street
Washington Pl.
Elysian Hotel
The Whitehall Hotel
Water Tower Place
Ritz-Carlton
Northwestern University

CONNORS PARK
Chicago Water Tower
Park Hyatt
Pumping Station
SENECA PARK
Museum of Contemporary Art
LAKE SHORE PARK

Ⓙ Chicago
W. Chicago Avenue
East Chicago Avenue

Holy Name Cathedral
Giordano's
Affinia
C-View Lounge
Northwestern University
East Superior Street

West Huron Street
Hotel Felix
Peninsula Chicago
The Allerton Magnificent Mile
East Huron Street

Gino's East
Dana Hotel and Spa
St James Cathedral
East Erie Street
N. Fairbanks Court

West Erie Street
Vertigo Sky Lounge
Magnificent Mile
N. St Clair St

W. Ontario Street
Red Head Piano Bar
Quartino
WaterShed
Sayat Nova
East Ontario Street
N. McClurg Court

Weird Chicago
The James
Vosges Haut-Chocolat
East Ohio Street

W. Ohio Street
Ohio Street
East

W. Grand Avenue
Blue Chicago
Hilton Garden Inn Chicago Magnificent Mile
The Shops at Northbridge
InterContinental Chicago
Eno
STREETERVILLE
Fox & Obel

West Illinois Street
XOCO
Grand Street
Conrad Chicago
Bobby's Bike Hike

Brown Line
Curio
Merchandise Mart
Jazz Record Mart
The Purple Pig
Tribune Tower
OGDEN PLAZA
East North Water St

West Kinzie Street
Bin 36
East Hubbard Street
Wrigley Building
N. Park Dr
N. Columbus Dr

Merchandise Mart
Trump International Hotel & Tower Chicago
Wrigley Plaza
site of Jean Baptiste Point Du Sable House
Chicago

site of Fort Dearborn
Whacker Drive

60
Ⓐ
Ⓑ
Ⓒ
Ⓓ

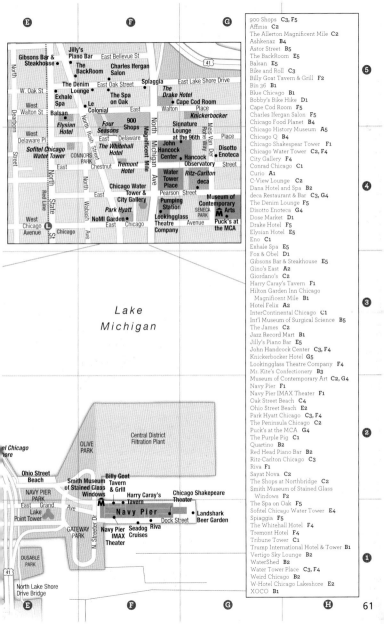

E   F   G

Map labels:

Jilly's Piano Bar
East Bellevue St
Gibsons Bar & Steakhouse
The BackRoom
Charles Ifergan Salon
Spiaggia
East Oak Street
The Denim Lounge
East Lake Shore Drive
W. Oak St
Exhale Spa
The Spa on Oak
The Drake Hotel
West Walton St
Balsan
Le Colonial
East Walton
Cape Cod Room
Place
Knickerbocker
Elysian Hotel
Four Seasons
900 Shops
East Delaware
Signature Lounge at the 96th Fl.
West Delaware Pl
Magnificent Mile
The Whitehall Hotel
John Hancock Center
Hancock Observatory
Disotto Enoteca
CONNORS PARK
East Chestnut
Tremont Hotel
Ritz-Carlton deca
East Pearson Street
Chicago Water Tower & City Gallery
Water Tower Place
Museum of Contemporary Arts
North State Red Line
Park Hyatt
Pumping Station
SENECA PARK
West Chicago Avenue
NoMI Garden
Lookingglass Theatre Company
Puck's at the MCA
Chicago Ave
East Chicago Avenue

Lake Michigan

el Chicago hore
Ohio Street Beach
NAVY PIER PARK
East Grand Ave
Lake Point Tower
Smith Museum of Stained Glass Windows
Billy Goat Tavern & Grill
Central District Filtration Plant
OLIVE PARK
Harry Caray's Tavern
Chicago Shakespeare Theater
Navy Pier
Landshark Beer Garden
Dock Street
Riva
GATEWAY PARK
Navy Pier IMAX Theater
Seadog Cruises
DUSABLE PARK
41
North Lake Shore Drive Bridge

E   F   G   H

Stroll along the flower-lined **Magnificent Mile**, site of 200 restaurants and over 450 shops

The Magnificent Mile – or Mag Mile, as it's called locally – is found on the city's near north side, close to Chicago's bustling Loop and the so-called 'Viagra Triangle' of Rush Street. One of the city's most frequented and prestigious thoroughfares, it's a visitor's dream, one filled with a vast collection of upscale shops, elegant hotels, fine and casual restaurants, and historic, landmark architecture. Part of Daniel Burnham's Plan of Chicago, the Mag Mile arose in the 1920s in an effort to revamp then factory-riddled Pine Street. After the Great Depression and World War II, most of the properties were presided over by developer Arthur Rubloff and his New York partner, William Zeckendorf, who laid claim to its destiny. Now the epitome of what a high-rent district is meant to be, it oozes luxury while housing some of the world's tallest structures.

Keep your eyes open while exploring, as Mag Mile icons are plentiful, starting with **Water Tower Place** (835 N. Michigan Avenue; tel: 312-440-3166), which houses stores from Betsey Johnson to American Girl Place and Sassoon. Accommodations around these parts are noteworthy, too, from the regal Drake Hotel, stylish Ritz-Carlton Chicago, and Four Seasons Hotel Chicago, to the sedate Park Hyatt. History buffs find plenty to love as well in the **home-site of Jean Baptiste Point Du Sable** (401 N. Michigan Avenue) *(p.149)*, the site of **Fort Dearborn** (North Michigan Avenue and East Wacker Drive), and the castle-like **Chicago Water Tower and Pumping Station** (806 N. Michigan Avenue), built from Joliet limestone. Inside this William W. Boyington-designed building, **City Gallery** (806 N. Michigan Avenue; tel: 312-742-0808; free) hosts Chicago-centric photography exhibits.

After perusing what's hung, you're poised for a spree at the **900 Shops** (900 N. Michigan Avenue; tel: 312-915-3916), anchored by Bloomingdale's and **The Shops at Northbridge** (520 N. Michigan Avenue; tel: 312-327-2300), where it's easy – blissful, in fact – to pass an afternoon at the Nordstrom shoe department. Before you tire out, ascend 1,000 feet to the **Hancock Observatory** (94th floor, John Hancock Center, 875 N. Michigan Avenue; tel: 888-875-8439; charge)

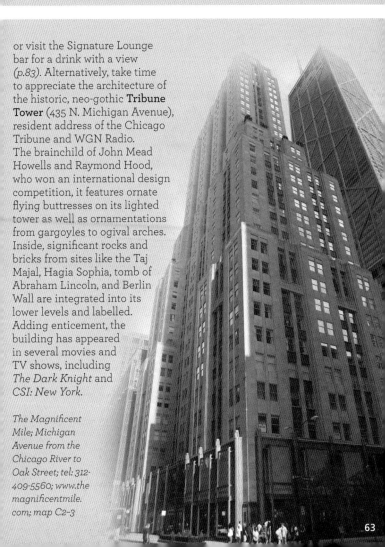

or visit the Signature Lounge bar for a drink with a view (*p.83*). Alternatively, take time to appreciate the architecture of the historic, neo-gothic **Tribune Tower** (435 N. Michigan Avenue), resident address of the Chicago Tribune and WGN Radio. The brainchild of John Mead Howells and Raymond Hood, who won an international design competition, it features ornate flying buttresses on its lighted tower as well as ornamentations from gargoyles to ogival arches. Inside, significant rocks and bricks from sites like the Taj Majal, Hagia Sophia, tomb of Abraham Lincoln, and Berlin Wall are integrated into its lower levels and labelled. Adding enticement, the building has appeared in several movies and TV shows, including *The Dark Knight* and *CSI: New York*.

The Magnificent Mile; Michigan Avenue from the Chicago River to Oak Street; tel: 312-409-5560; www.the magnificentmile. com; map C2-3

Catch some rays at **Oak Street Beach**

It's hard to believe that sun-drenched **Oak Street Beach** arrived by accident, but it's true. Situated on North Lake Shore Drive along Lake Michigan from 1550 to 500 North Lake Shore Drive, it developed after a shipping pier – that had been erected at the river – caused silt build-up, and sand washed to the north end of Streeterville. Today this arc of sand is popular with residents, suburbanites, and tourists when summer arrives, and it is now framed by concrete north and south running paths, which connect Ohio Street and North Avenue Beaches. Meanwhile, for those who want to just lounge the day away in the sun and prefer to do something active, **Bike and Roll** has several locations in Chicago and rents everything from tandems and quadcycles to handcycles, children's bikes, attachable wagons, and infant seats on site.

Then again, you can always go for a **swim** – it's permitted when lifeguards are on duty. However, do remember that swimming is subject to water conditions: a green flag means it's safe to swim, while a yellow flag suggests proceeding with caution and a red flag indicates hazardous conditions.

Take note that the beach is a particularly popular perch during shoreline festivities, such as the annual **Air and Water Show**, when you can expect to share space with the masses.

Oak Street Beach; 1000 N. Lake Shore Drive; tel: 312-742-5121; www.chicagoparkdistrict.com; free; map C4
Bike and Roll Chicago; Lake Shore Drive at Oak Street; tel: 312-729-1000; www.bikeandroll.com/chicago; daily, weather permitting, 10am–6pm Memorial Day–Labor Day; charge; map C3

Sup cocktails at Vertigo Sky Lounge, whatever the weather

Perched prettily on the 26th floor rooftop of the Dana hotel and spa, **Vertigo Sky Lounge** is a sweeping, glass-encased, low-lit lounge kitted out with curvaceous leather seating, sleek side tables, and plush, high-backed chairs overlooking the stunning skyline to the north, south, and east. Thumping, conversation-friendly beats are spun by DJs nightly, while cocktails are dispensed by scantily clad servers with rolling beverage carts. Outside, the terrace – which has its own modular seating – is hung with balls of light and fitted with fire pits. It's also the site of a luminescent, winter-only **Fire and Ice** bar; crafted from 3,000 pounds of ice, it turns out boozy snow cones and flaming shots that warm you up – whatever the temperatures. Fortunately, for those who are less-enamored with the outdoor elements, robes and fur blankets are on hand.

A menu of classic and tweaked cocktails – coupled with an Asian-tinged selection of small plates – rounds out the experience. Be sure to check out the unisex bathroom – its porthole window makes using the facilities an appealing proposition. Since the River North spot is regularly the sight of celebrity bashes, keep your

eyes trained on the crowd – you never know who you might see. It's also why you should call ahead: sometimes the pad is closed for private gatherings. Since you will already be dressed to impress, head on to see a set at wee-hours **Red Head Piano Bar**, a live cabaret that's decked with sheet music and playbills from yesteryear.

Dana hotel and spa; 2 W. Erie Street; tel: 312-202-6060; www. vertigoskylounge.com; Mon–Wed 5pm–1am, Thur 5pm–2am, Fri noon–2am, Sat noon–3am, Sun noon–midnight; map B2 Red Head Piano Bar; 16 W. Ontario Street; tel: 312-640-1000; redhead pianobar.com; Sat 7pm–5am, Sun–Fri 7pm–4am; map B2

Experience **First Fridays** at the **Museum of Contemporary Art**

The **Museum of Contemporary Art**, or MCA, dates back to 1967 when it opened as a modern art complement to the collection at the Art Institute of Chicago *(p.91)*. Although it began by focusing on temporary exhibitions, it soon acquired permanent work. Today, it features not only curated shows but also performances and educational programming – from talks to discussions and artist-led workshops – for all ages.

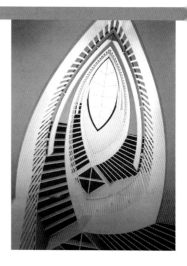

The museum's collection is significant, with visual art from 1945 to today, encompassing the genres of minimalism, surrealism, and conceptual photography. It's where you can see Andy Warhol's *Campbell's Soup Cans II* and works by Marcel Duchamp, Francis Bacon, Alexander Calder, and Jasper Johns. The second Saturday of each month, from 11am–3pm, offers hands-on learning stations for families, while first Wednesday 'stroller tours,' held from early June until early September at 11.30am, are perfect for those with tots.

On the other side of the spectrum, DJ-backed happy hour-themed **first Fridays** (held, unsurprsingly, on the first Friday of the month) feature a cash bar pouring specialty cocktails, the work of emerging Chicago artists to admire, live entertainment, and bites from Wolfgang Puck's in-house **Puck's at the MCA**.

In summer, there's also a farmers' market on Tuesday mornings. And on Tuesday evenings at 5.30pm, the terrace hosts performances by Chicago jazz musicians along with a buffet of locally grown grub.

Museum of Contemporary Art; 220 E. Chicago Avenue; tel: 312-397-4010; www.mcachicago.org; Tue 10am–8pm, Wed-Sun 10am–5pm; free Tue, charge otherwise; map C2, G4

Take a narrated, **food-themed walking tour** with **Chicago Food Planet**

Get an authentic taste of Chicago's culinary community during a walking tour with **Chicago Food Planet**. Its guides reveal tasty treats citywide, from classics to hidden gems with mom-and-pop appeal. Its near north leg unearths edibles in the Gold Coast area, from specialty food stores to ethnic eateries. Stop at the historic **Ashkenaz** deli, known for its pastrami and corned beef sandwiches on rye as well as matzo ball soup. Moving on, swing by a Polish bakery, where macaroons and almond croissants have the potential to expand waistlines. Then visit a Chicago-style pizzeria for a taste of deep-dish delights. Trekkers will also pay visits to spice and loose-leaf tea merchants and the city's oldest confectioner, all while soaking up tree-lined streets, lushly landscaped parks, and architectural masterpieces. Plan on purchasing tickets in advance, and expect to spend up to 3½ hours on foot during rain, sunshine, or teeth-chattering snow.

Other tours to check out include a Bucktown/Wicker Park excursion to six restaurants, among them a Chicago-style hot dog stand, and a Chinatown tour exploring Mandarin, Szechuan, and Canton cuisines, including everything from dim sum to a Peking duck dinner.

Alternatively, sweet-seekers might consider joining an excursion with **Chicago Chocolate Tours** (visit 900 N. Michigan Avenue; tel: 312-929-2939; map C3), which journeys to a handful of the city's favorite chocolate cafes, bakeries, and stores, such as More Cupcakes, Hendrickx Belgian Bread Crafter, and Teuscher Chocolates. Then again, you could always just pop into home-grown **Vosges Haut-Chocolat** (520 N. Michigan Avenue; tel: 312-644-9450; map C2), guide-free. It's known for its exotic truffles and candy bars, which include bacon-chocolate, absinthe, and balsamico varieties.

Rush and Division Streets (exact meeting location provided with ticket purchase); tel: 800-979-3370; www. chicagofoodplanet.com; 11am daily; charge; map B4

Revel in the **glamour** of the **Gold Coast**, home to **Astor Street**'s landmark architecture

Home to some of Chicago's most affluent addresses, the **Gold Coast** is graced with many landmarks that are listed on the National Register of Historical Places, making this an ideal area for architecture fans to explore. Potter Palmer's duplex is now a private residence at 33 E. Division Street, while this area was also home to John Wellborn Root, Frank Lloyd Wright, and Irma Phillips, the 'mother of the soap opera.' Additionally, the Gold Coast is the site of the **Astor Street** district, situated in the 1200–1600 blocks of Astor Street and its cross streets. Constructed over the course of 60 years, this area comprises several stunning 19th-century homes, fashioned in a variety of historical revival styles, that mingle with high-rise 20th-century apartments and townhouses. Thick canopies of trees create a hushed atmosphere that make it easy to envisage the affluent world of the late 19th-century elite.

One excellent surviving structure at the northern end of the district is the **Archbishop's Residence**, the home of the leader of the city's Catholic diocese. A brick structure studded with towers, turrets, and chimneys, it is set apart from its neighbors by a wide lawn. Just a few blocks south is a building in which no doubt many activities occurred that the Catholic church would frown on: the **Playboy Mansion**, where magazine publisher Hugh Hefner lived and worked until he left for Los Angeles in the 1980s.

Continue on and do some window-shopping on **Oak Street**, lined with posh stores. The block between Michigan and Rush is the city's most glittering **shopping** area, with designer and independent boutiques tucked into elegant townhouses.

If you're looking to continue the luxury theme, reserve a table at jackets-required **Spiaggia** (980 N. Michigan Avenue, 2nd fl.; tel: 312-280-2750), a fancy Italian dining room where you'll be met with melt-in-the-mouth pasta and an amazing view of Lake Michigan. Slightly more budget-friendly is its sibling **Café Spiaggia**, or for something different, visit **Sayat Nova** (157 E. Ohio Street; tel: 312-644-9159; map C2), a hidden-feeling Armenian spot in Streeterville. Its menu tempts with lentil soup, lamb couscous, and many kebabs.

Astor Street; from Schiller Street to North Avenue; map B5

Grab some tickets for a **performance** at **Lookingglass Theatre Company**

Located in the Streeterville neighborhood within the **Water Tower Water Works**, the Tony Award-winning, ensemble-based **Lookingglass Theatre Company** was founded in the late 1980s by a collective that includes *Friends* star David Schwimmer. Its first production was the David Kersner-directed *Through the Lookingglass*, which took place at Jones Residential College on the Northwestern University campus. Its current, permanent facility, secured in 2003, is a customizable black-box style space with a removable balcony and seating for up to 270. Productions range from original plays to adaptations, and many of them wind up recipients of Jeff Awards, which acknowledge excellence in Chicago-area theater.

For the best of both worlds when you're traveling with kids, check out something from its family series. Children have the chance to participate in a workshop with crafts, storytelling, and snacks, leaving parents free to watch a show without distraction.

If you time it right, you may also catch the **Chicago Underground Film Festival** (Gene Siskel Film Center, 164 N. State Street; tel: 312-846-2600). Typically held in June, it highlights independent and experimental local and international flicks, followed by live concerts and festive soirees.

Lookingglass Theatre Company; 821 N. Michigan Avenue; tel: 312-337-0665; www.lookingglasstheatre.org; charge; map F4

THEATER MENUS
Post performance, sip cocktails at sky-high **C-View lounge** (Affinia Chicago, 166 E. Superior Street; tel: 312-523-0923; map C2), sun-drenched **NoMI Garden** (Park Hyatt, 800 N. Michigan Avenue; tel: 312-239-4030; map F4), or **deca Restaurant + Bar** (Ritz-Carlton Chicago, 160 E. Pearson St; tel: 312-573-5160; map C3, G4), where seafood towers are theatrical in their own right.

Go for an **extreme ride** aboard a sightseeing speedboat with **Seadog Cruises**

Visitors flock to **Navy Pier**, a 50-acre mecca of parks, gardens, and entertainment on the shores of Lake Michigan. It's the site of countless attractions – an iconic Ferris wheel, mirrored funhouse maze, miniature golf course, and a musical carousel, to name a few – and also the launching pad for **Segway tours**, which ramble through Olive Park, Oak Street Beach, and Lincoln Park, continuing to the Drake Hotel, Mies van der Rohe's condominiums, and the campuses of Northwestern University.

Fun those these are, it would be a shame to overlook the pier's sightseeing cruises. There's a 148-foot, four-masted schooner,

plus several dinner cruises and private charters to choose from. For the most exciting experience, though, hop aboard the 30-minute **Seadog Extreme Thrill Ride**, a scream–fest with 180- and 360-degree spins, zigzag runs, and breathtaking twists and turns.

Those looking for something a bit more low-key should consider taking one of the company's extended, narrated **fireworks cruises**, which set out on Wednesday and Saturday nights and afford panoramic, glinting skyline views. There's also a 75-minute **architectural cruise** with highlights such as the Chicago River, locks and bridges, Marina City, the Merchandise Mart, and the Willis Tower.

After disembarking, head to the **Landshark** beer garden, a popular place for a tipple on balmy days, especially when live entertainment is scheduled. Also, consider wandering through the pier's Gateway Park and along Dock Street when **Navy Pier Walk** showcases public art installations.

Seadog Cruises; Navy Pier, 600 E. Grand Avenue; tel: 888-636-7737; www. seadogcruises.com; daily in season at noon, 1pm, 2pm and 4pm; charge; map F1

Hide away while taking in some jazz at **WaterShed**, a vintage-inspired **drinking den**

A subterranean River North lair located beneath **Pops for Champagne** – itself a long-standing and hugely popular bubbly bar – **WaterShed** exudes a parlor-like feel but maintains a devotion to beer, wine and spirits from the Great Lakes region. Wrapped with rustic limestone walls, high-backed booths, and groups of upholstered seating, it serves classic cocktails – modernized just so – including a Moscow Mule with Crop cucumber vodka, Koval ginger, lime, and ginger beer, and the Chicago Fizz, a blend of New Holland Michigan Rum, tawny port, lemon, egg whites, and club soda. The tipples are easy to throw back, so turn to beyond-basic small plates until late, be it spaetzle with raised radishes, brown butter, Dijon, and dill, or duck pastrami and roasted bone marrow with pickled red onion and garlic confit. Fancy yourself more of a grazer? The array of charcuterie and cheeses are hardly mere afterthoughts.

Every bit as hidden-feeling is cash-only **Curio**. Tucked beneath **Gilt Bar**, it has *tête-à-tête* written all over it, what with its candlelit setting, leather banquettes, and hand-crafted, speakeasy sips, that are made to be enjoyed over leisurely conversations between couples and small groups. Behind this sexy boîte is Brendan Sodikoff, who spent time working with Thomas Keller and Alain Ducasse.

WaterShed; 601 N. State Street; tel: 312-266-4932; www.watershedbar.com; Mon–Sat 5pm–2am; map B2
Curio; 230 W. Kinzie Street, Lower level; tel: 312-464-9544; www.giltbarchicago.com; Thur–Sat 7pm–2am; map A1

Wheel your way through **President Barack Obama's neighborhood**

Using Streeterville as its launching pad, **Bobby's Bike Hike** heads to the 44th President's stomping grounds in Hyde Park, complete with a cruise past his residence. All the while, participants wheel through the historically and culturally rich neighborhood, home to Jackson Park, the Museum of Science and Industry, and the site of the 1893 World's Columbian Exposition. Continuing through the University of Chicago campus, the journey stops at the Rockefeller Chapel, the Nuclear Sculpture, and Frank Lloyd Wright's Robie House. The four-hour adventure follows a 23-mile course, one that also showcases the scenic Japanese Gardens.

Other tours to watch for from the crew include 'bikes, bites & brews,' which brakes for pizza, hot dogs, cupcakes, and – as the name implies – beer, as well as night-time city lights and lakefront neighborhoods tours that coast past Oprah's house, the Playboy mansion (p.69), and Lincoln Park Zoo (p.49). Since that may not be right for everyone, you can always opt for an intimate, entertaining kid's edition bike excursion. The trip includes a fountain coin-toss and lakefront trail route, scheduled before the sun gets too hot. Bobby's also provides bike rentals complete with helmets and maps at points throughout Chicago.

As another plus, small group tours can be conducted in languages from Portuguese to Russian, German, French, Dutch, Italian, and Spanish. Child and infant seats, trailers and tag-a-longs should be requested in advance when tickets are purchased.

Bobby's Bike Hike; Historic Hyde Park Tour, 465 N. McClurg Court; tel: 312-915-0995; www.bobbysbikehike.com; Fri–Sun 8.30am; charge; map D1

Seek out the surprisingly chill **Smith Museum of Stained Glass Windows** at **Navy Pier**

It'd be easy to spend the day at family-oriented **Navy Pier**, whether it's riding the rides in Pier Park, shopping, or trying your hand at the remote controlled boats. Countless free shows – plus jugglers, magicians, and marching bands – mean no one gets bored, whatever their age. Souvenir-type shopping is plentiful – whether for t-shirts, branded accessories, or off-kilter gifts – and options for eating and drinking are endless. Grab a sandwich and see museum-caliber sports memorabilia at **Harry Caray's Tavern**; (700 E. Grand Avenue; tel: 312-527-9700); indulge in fresh catches at seafooder **Riva** (700 E. Grand Avenue; tel: 312-644-7482); or pick up a 'cheezborger' at **Billy Goat Tavern & Grill** (700 E.

Grand Avenue; tel: 312-670-8789), made famous by the 'Saturday Night Live' skit.

The real gem of a find here, though, is the **Smith Museum of Stained Glass Windows**. The 800ft-long gallery – remote-feeling and situated along the lower level terraces of Festival Hall – is more than just a pretty sight. It also offers insight into Chicago's cultural, artistic, and ethnic past. The windows – Victorian, Prairie, Modern, or Contemporary in style – come from local residential, commercial, and religious buildings. Included in the display is over a dozen Louis Comfort Tiffany creations. Also on show are window works from John LaFarge and Chicago artists Ed Paschke and Roger Brown. There's even a cool version crafted from soda bottles. Take your time looking and notice the evolution of aesthetics and architectural styles, including those favored by European immigrants and commercial and cultural institutions from 1870 until the present.

Navy Pier; 600 E. Grand Avenue; tel: 312-595-7437; Sun–Thur 10am–8pm, Fri–Sat 10am–10pm; free; map F2

Attend a **wine-tasting class** or just savor house-curated keg wine at **Eno**

Situated in the InterContinental Chicago along the Mag Mile, **Eno** embraces the finer things in life: wine, chocolate, and cheese from global, artisanal producers. Petite, welcoming, and free of pretension, it has a vast, whimsically described wine list of bottled and by-the-glass selections that make narrowing down choices an adventure. It also proffers 26-bottle-sized keg wines, which limit the carbon footprint of production and consumption, are affordable, and result from custom blending by Wine Director Scott Harney.

Cheese and chocolate flights are impossible-to-resist companions. The former – grouped by region or theme – include fruit mostarda, Marcona almonds, black olives, and slices of baguette and nut bread. Chocolate flights, on the other hand, might revolve around fleur de sel, bittersweet flavors, or aromatic spices.

Bringing the experience down to earth, wine education classes are on regular rotation, both here and at its location in the Fairmont Chicago. Gatherings may reveal how to pair grilled fare with Zinfandel; what's a match for Nebbiolo, Petite Sirah, and Sangiovese; or the pleasures of aromatic, patio-friendly whites.

Afterwards, if you find yourself in need of something substantial in the food department, get a steak at **Gibsons Bar & Steakhouse** (1028 N. Rush Street; tel: 312-266-8999; map E5), gussied up barbecue at **Chicago Q** (1160 N. Dearborn Street; tel: 312-642-1160; map B4), or raw bar selections and house-cured charcuterie at **Balsan** (Elysian Hotel, 11 E. Walton Street; tel 312-646-1400; map E5).

Eno; InterContinental Chicago, 505 N. Michigan Avenue; www.enowinerooms. com; tel: 312-321-8738; Mon-Thur 4pm-midnight, Fri-Sat 1pm-1am, Sun 1-10pm; map E1

Learn about Chicago's prolific **underbelly** during a **Weird Chicago Tour**

There are few better ways to acquaint yourself with Chicago than to take an entertaining, if off-kilter, **Weird Chicago** tour to learn of the ghouls, ghosts, and gangsters that called the city home. But be forewarned: if it's staid haunts you're looking for, you'd be better served elsewhere. Featuring everything from serial killer, red light district, and 'Devil in the White City'-themed excursions, it also hosts a public enemies-themed exploration of John Dillinger that includes stops at his North Side hideouts and the brothel of Anna Sage. History buffs might also book 'Blood, Guns & Valentines,' a crime tour stopping at gangland sites, spots synonymous with Al Capone, the location of the Luetgert Sausage vat murder, and the site where the St Valentine's Day Massacre occurred. From weird and haunted locales to colorful women of Chicago and supernatural occurrences, the guides help to reveal all.

Then again, if you're looking for something a bit more mainstream or less bloodthirsty, don't despair. You can entertain options like the 'Be-Bop, Blues & The Beatles' tour, which reveals Chicago's musical history, or a weird pub-crawl for those who are 21-plus. Planning on heading to Chicago around Halloween? Consider a tour as a fittingly spooktacular option.

Most of the bus-bound gatherings are three hours long and should be reserved in advance; note that children under the age of 10 are not allowed.

Weird Chicago tours; departing by bus from Hard Rock Café, 63 W. Ontario Street, Chicago, IL 60654; tel: 888-446-7859; www.weirdchicago.com; times and prices vary; map B2

Solve all your **jeans woes** at **The Denim Lounge**, then indulge in some personal **pampering**

Let's face it: shopping for jeans is a tear-inducing experience at worst, an exercise in patience at best. That's where high-end **The Denim Lounge** comes in. Featuring about two-dozen lines in every style imaginable – including slim, straight-legs by Hudson for guys and flares from DL1961 for gals – it also stocks a wide array of things to go with. Troll the racks for lace Ella Moss tees, oversized tunics from LinQ and Bordeaux's 'marbled,' racer-back camis. Then finish looks with a belt or clutch.

If you're brave, reap the rewards of the shop's 'butt cam,' which projects a 360-degree image of your backside on a monitor. Yes, it sounds harrowing – but it does help you see what shapes work best for you. On a more soothing note, girls' nights out – complete with discounts and cocktails – are often held here.

Whether you're solo or enjoying some time with a pal, follow shopping for your perfect denims with some pampering time. You could get a hairdo at **Charles Ifergan Salon** (106 E. Oak Street; tel. 312-642-4484; map F5), a mani-pedi at **Exhale Spa** (945 N. State Street; tel: 312-753-6500; map E5), or indulge in a massage at **The Spa on Oak** (67 E. Oak Street; tel: 312-280-6283; map F5).

And for delicious tastes that won't have you bursting out of your jeans, head to southeast Asia by way of **Le Colonial** (937 N. Rush Street; tel: 312-255-0088; map F5), a palm-frocked spot for Vietnamese fare, like sugar cane-speared shrimp with angel hair noodles, lettuce, mint, and peanut sauce.

The Denim Lounge; 43 E. Oak Street; tel: 312-642-6403; www.madisonand friends.com/denimlounge; Mon-Sat 10am-6.30pm, Sun 11am–5pm; map F5

Eat lots of swine while sipping cost-conscious wine at tucked-away **The Purple Pig**

A powerhouse line-up backs **The Purple Pig**, complete with chef Jimmy Bannos Jr. in the kitchen. This small and busy restaurant, which specializes in small plates, is known for its boldly flavored, porky delights, including those made from pigs' less-utilized parts. Seating is at a premium – most is either communal or found at the White Carrera marble-topped bar – but no one seems to mind as they sit amid warm, Edison bulb-lit surrounds, accented with tiles, wine barrels and ceramic versions of its namesake, and a patio with wine barrel tabletops, where locals linger over bowls of inventively flavored soft-serve ice cream during warmer months.

Starring on the Mediterranean-inflected menu – where even the almonds are fried in pork fat – is the fried egg-topped pig's ear with crisp kale and pickled cherry peppers. Smears are furthered by tangy braised pig's tail, milk-braised pork shoulder, and excellent fried, chorizo-stuffed olives. These accompany the Euro-bent cellar selections, 50 of which ring in at under $40 and can be procured by the glass, quartino, or half bottle. Located on the Mag Mile, it's an ideal mid- or post-shopping pit stop with a decidedly convivial and hip flavor. Afterward, if you need a sweet infusion, indulge in hot chocolate, *caldos* and *tortas* at **XOCO**, Rick Bayless' matchbox-sized must.

Want to skip the crowds entirely at lunchtime? Find fixings for a fantastic picnic at gourmet grocer **Fox & Obel** instead.

The Purple Pig; 500 N. Michigan Avenue; tel: 312-464-1744; www.thepurplepigchicago.com; Sun–Thur 11.30am–midnight, Fri–Sat 11.30am–2am; map C1
XOCO; 449 N. Clark Street; tel: 312-334-3688; www.rickbayless.com; Tue–Thur 8am–9pm, Fri–Sat 8am–10pm; map B1
Fox & Obel; 401 E. Illinois Street; tel: 312-410-7301; www.fox-obel.com; daily 6am–midnight; map D1

Try not to freak out at the **International Museum of Surgical Science**

Nestled into a 1917 mansion with Lake Michigan views, **International Museum of Surgical Science** is an artifact-laden fear-fest, focusing on the history and advancement of medicine and surgery over time. Whether it's a traveling exhibit of preserved, whole-body organ specimens, paintings of primitive healing practices, or artifacts from an Austrian amputation – including a saw with a reversible blade – this museum isn't exactly for the faint of heart. Other finds over the four-storeys include a manuscript collection of over 650 papers and letters from the likes of Florence Nightingale; prints, sculptures and portraits that depict medical figures, procedures, and happenings in an ornate, grand hall on the second floor; and tools and relics, from X-rays to acupuncture implements. Learn of a trephining of the cranium that occurred in prehistoric Peru, and see how human dissection might have been performed in the Middle Ages. Then, buy postcard versions and models in the gift shop.

Regularly hosted exhibitions focus on modern-day matters, such as stem cell research, plastic surgery, or chromatherapy, keeping the experience relevant to the present day. Also upping the ante are self-guided tours in topics like advances in medicine or anatomy and physiology.

Groups of visitors can also partake in an interactive 'amputation,' which requires advance registration.

International Museum of Surgical Science; 1524 N. Lake Shore Drive; tel: 312-642-6502; www.imss.org; Tue–Fri 10am–5pm, Sat 10am–9pm, Sun noon–5pm; charge; map B5

Soak up some blues at the veritable **Blue Chicago**, or kick back to jazz at **Jilly's Piano Bar**

in for some smooth tunes and people-watching; both are found in spades. When seats are a hot commodity, there's always jazz at rowdy **The BackRoom**, a dark, couple-populated haunt with exposed brick walls. Depending on your preference, sit on the main floor, or grab a seat on the upstairs balcony with a bird's eye view of the stage.

Blue Chicago; 536 N. Clark Street; tel: 312-661-0100; www.bluechicago.com; Sun–Fri 8pm–1.30am, Sat 8pm–2.30am; charge; map B1
Jilly's Piano Bar; 1007 N. Rush Street; tel: 312-664-1001; www.jillyschicago. com; Sun–Fri 4pm–2am, Sat 4pm–3am; no cover; map E5
The BackRoom; 1007 N. Rush Street; tel: 312-751-2433; www.backroomchicago. com; Sun–Fri 8pm–2am, Sat 8pm–3am; charge; map E5

Chicago's blues history is longstanding. At **Blue Chicago**, you can catch local acts – many of them strong female vocalists – keeping the tradition alive. Loaded with character, the inexpensive drinks and welcoming vibe garners local love, especially given there are regulars on rotation like The Shirley Johnson Blues Band and the JW Williams Blues Band.

Whenever you visit, consider swinging by **Jilly's Piano Bar**, an intimate Rush and Division staple where jazz trios, Rat Pack fanatics and piano players perform. Order a strong appletini or small-batch bourbon and settle

> ### CHICAGO BLUES FEST
> Blues fans visiting in June should not miss the city's legendary, three-day **Chicago Blues Fest** (Grant Park, Jackson Boulevard and Columbus Drive; tel: 312-744-3316; p.87 map G4), held in Grant Park. Billed as the largest free blues festival in the world, past luminaries included Bonnie Raitt, Ray Charles and B.B. King as well as Buddy Guy and Bo Diddley.

Explore the city through the eyes of the **Chicago History Museum**

Whether you participate in one of their historical walking tours or trolley-based pub-crawls, or learn of local lore, the **Chicago History Museum** is a destination unto itself. Housing over 22 million artifacts, its collection covers everything from decorative and industrial arts to paintings, sculpture, prints, and photographs. There are architectural drawings, along with models and fragments of buildings, among them parts of the Francisco Terrace Apartments designed by Frank Lloyd Wright. Fashionistas will appreciate the costumes and textiles section, which houses many garments made by Chicago milliners and dressmakers. It's also where you'll find an old Michael Jordan kit and suits worn by George Washington and John Adams.

Adding depth, temporary exhibitions delve into topics like unexpected history, Chinatown, or Abraham Lincoln. There's an on-site research center, too, where you'll find maps, atlases, and a bevy of prints and published materials that have stood the test of time. On your way out, don't forget to stop at the museum shop – it's stocked with vintage Chicago travel posters, books, and magazines relating to the city and board games and puzzles that do the Midwest proud. You'll also find cool odds and ends, like kiln-fired salt and pepper shakers inspired by Frank Lloyd Wright, picture frames adorned with Louis Sullivan-style balusters, and replica Brown Line 'L' train cars.

Chicago History Museum; 1601 N. Clark Street; tel: 312-642-4600; www. chicagohs.org; Mon–Sat 9.30am– 4.30pm, Sun noon–5pm; charge; map A5

Tame your inner shrew during a performance at
Chicago Shakespeare Theater

Located on Navy Pier, the 510-seat **Chicago Shakespeare Theater** – a Regional Theatre Tony Award winner – affords a performance fix 48 weeks of the year. At center stage is the theater's subscription series, which draws from the canon of Shakespeare's works while showcasing additional, touted plays from the past and present. Members of the audience can gain insight into what they've seen – be it a play's historical context or political issues – during lectures from lit-wise scholars and other book discussions. Alternatively, its World Stage series highlights touring shows, and its New Classics push boundaries and shed new light on classical plays. And despite the place's literary propensity, pretension is kept to a minimum, while families are treated to abridged shows, specifically designed to engage and intrigue young ones.

While you're in the area, swing by the historic **Cape Cod Room** for seafood (140 E. Walton Pl.; tel; 312-787-2200), sip wine at **Quartino** (626 N. State Street; tel: 312-698-5000) or **Bin 36** (339 N. Dearborn Street; tel: 312-755-9463); or watch a movie at the **Navy Pier IMAX Theater** (600 E. Grand Avenue; tel: 312-595-5629) – it's outfitted with a soaring, six-story flat screen showing crowd-pleasing movies.

Then again, you could always take a stroll and see the **twin Ludwig Mies van der Rohe towers** at 860 N. Lake Shore Drive, take a peek at the exterior of the architect's home at 200 E. Pearson Street or simply gaze out at the **lighthouse** at Chicago Harbor, the only one surviving in the city and one of two in Illinois.

Chicago Shakespeare Theater; Navy Pier, 800 E. Grand Avenue; tel: 312-595-5600; www.chicagoshakes.com; times and prices vary; map F1

Make time for **romance** at **DiSotto Enoteca**

Hidden beneath Francesca's on Chestnut, late-night **DiSotto Enoteca** is an intimate, chat-friendly Gold Coast gem with a small plates-meets-antipasti bent and an exposed brick setting with cave-like appeal. Inside, find couples canoodling over bruschetta in versions such as pear, *Taleggio*, and toasted pistachio. Join in by ordering some ricotta and honeycomb spread and customized cheese and salumi platters. Naturally, you'll want wines to go with; handily, three dozen are available by the glass.

In the event you seek something less subterranean for a rendezvous, revel in the twinkling, sky-high view from **Signature Lounge at the 96th**, situated on its namesake floor in the **John Hancock building**. There, skyscraper-themed cocktails, cognac, and top-shelf spirits are offered alongside a catch-all menu. Be sure to entertain its seasonal sips, which may include a tamarind pisco sour, hibiscus tea cocktail, or the Purple Haze, a commingling of rum and blueberry and passion fruit juices.

Since romance is on the menu, make it your mission to visit **Maude's Liquor Bar** for a nightcap. This pleasure den serves fabulous

French fare and 'smashes,' like the Smokey Violet with gin and crème de violette. Sit upstairs, where leather banquettes are particularly inviting – at least when they aren't tightly packed.

DiSotto Enoteca; 200 E. Chestnut Street; tel: 312-482-8800; www. miafrancesca.com; Sun–Thur 5pm–midnight, Fri–Sat 5pm–1am; map G4
Signature Lounge at the 96th; John Hancock Center, 875 N. Michigan Avenue; tel: 312-787-9596; www. signatureroom.com/Signature-Lounge; Sun–Thur 11am–12.30am, Fri–Sat 11am–1.30am; map C3, G4
Maude's Liquor Bar; 840 W. Randolph Street; tel: 312-243-9712; www. maudesliquorbar.com; Tue–Fri 4.45pm–2am, Sat 5.45pm–2am; map p.86 B4

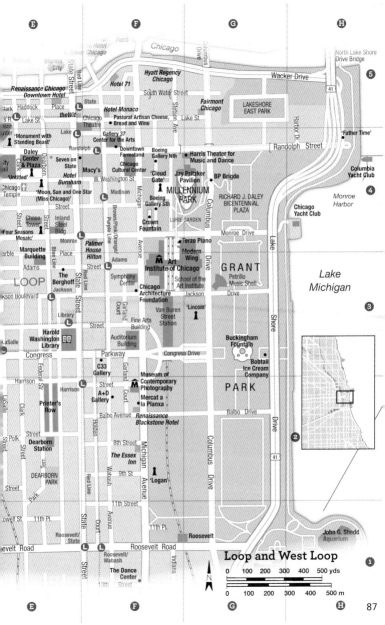

Loop and West Loop

| 0 | 100 | 200 | 300 | 400 | 500 yds |

| 0 | 100 | 200 | 300 | 400 | 500 m |

N

Catch a **classical concert**, while soaking up the skyline, during **Grant Park Music Festival** performances

Millennium Park is a year-round destination, though it's never more lively – or lovely – than during the fleeting summer months. Seasonally, the Grant Park Orchestra and Chorus put on a 10-week series of free, outdoor concerts and intensive rehearsals known as the **Grant Park Music Festival** at the architecturally dazzling, Frank Gehry-designed **Jay Pritzker Pavilion** in Millennium Park. Complimentary seating, which opens 90 minutes before performances, is available. However, those in the know prefer to soak up the setting (and skyline) from the lawn, all the while enjoying wine-bolstered picnics.

After the concert, take time to wander the landscaped parkland: it is filled with sculpture, architectural masterpieces, and even a theater. Among its most recognizable landmarks is *Cloud Gate* (commonly referred to as 'The Bean'), Anish Kapoor's elliptical, mirrored sculpture. Equally remarkable is the 50ft (15m) glass-block **Crown Fountain** – water towers by Jaume Plensa, which are projected with images of Chicagoans. The four-season, five-acre **Lurie Garden** is worth a gander as well; it nods to the city's roots as a flat marshland and its present-day role as a powerful, world-class city. Look for the 15ft-high (4½m) 'shoulder' hedge; it draws inspiration from **Carl Sandburg**, who depicted Chicago as the 'City of Big Shoulders.'

The secret-feeling space houses a garden, one intersected by a footbridge over calm water. It's also the site of garden events, such as nature-driven photo exhibitions. From there, make your way to the **Boeing Galleries**, located at the north and south sides of the park. You'll come across modern and contemporary art, all of it created by living artists. Note, too, Frank Gehry's winding, 925ft (282m) **BP Bridge** – made from brushed stainless steel panels that help block the sound of traffic at the Jay Pritzker Pavilion. The bridge serves as a memorable vantage point to view Grant Park, Lake Michigan, and the skyline. Because the park hosts over 500 free events annually, travelers should always be on the lookout for something more, like the scenic ice skating rink that appears each winter.

Grant Park is adjacent and you can continue your day there at leisure. Referred to as Chicago's 'front yard,' it's home to many of the city's major museums. Its focal point, though, is **Buckingham Fountain**. The flower-frocked park, shaded by age-old trees, is also the site of prominent city festivals, including **Taste of Chicago**, **Chicago Jazz Festival**, **Lollapalooza**, and **Chicago Blues Festival** (p.80).

There are numerous places to grab a bite nearby, including **Mercat a la Planxa** (638 S. Michigan Avenue; tel: 312-765-0524; map F2), for boldly flavored Catalan cuisine and creative cocktails. Cap off a banner day with scoops from native **Bobtail Ice Cream Company** (522 S. Lake Shore Drive; tel: 312-786-1014; map G3), which sets up a seasonal walk-up window in the park.

Jay Pritzker Pavilion; Millennium Park, 205 E. Randolph Street; tel: 312-742-7638; www.grantparkmusicfestival.com; various times; free; map G4
Grant Park; 337 Randolph Street; tel: 312-742-7648; www.chicagoparkdistrict. com; map G2–4

Take in a **bird's eye view** of the city at **Skydeck Chicago**

Located on the 103rd floor of **Willis Tower**, 1,353 ft (412m) above the street, **Skydeck Chicago** affords stunning, four-state views on clear days. The iconic, 110-story commercial building – designed by architects Skidmore, Owings and Merrill in the early 1970s – was quite the endeavor to construct. Honed from enough concrete to construct a five-mile (8km) -long, eight-lane highway, it houses 25 miles (40km) of plumbing and 1,500 miles (2,414km) of electric wiring. Dubbed the Sears Tower until 2009 when it was purchased by London-based insurance broker, the Willis Group, locals are hard-pressed to call it by any other name. At one time it was the tallest building in the world and it's still a popular destination for marriage proposals, as well for visitors from near and far, all of them collectively whisked to the pinnacle in multi-media-equipped elevators,

Of course, while the panorama through windows is unrivaled, nothing can ready you for the experience of stepping onto **The Ledge**, a glass platform that hovers four heart-thumping feet (1.2m) outside of the tower, above the Chicago River and Wacker Drive. Built by the building's original architecture firm, the glass-enclosed box has an all-but-invisible support system and clear, three-layer glass panels weighing in at 1,500lb (680kg) each. While here, take time to see Chicago-themed exhibits, and watch a movie detailing the tower's construction and highlighting other Chicago landmarks. Plan on arriving an hour before sunset to see daylight, twilight, and nighttime combined, and to catch the miniature streetscapes in every possible glow.

Skydeck Chicago; 233 S. Wacker Drive; tel: 312-875-9696; www.theskydeck. com; Apr–Sept 9am–10pm, Oct–Mar 10am–8pm; charge; map D3

Visit the stunning, sunlight-drenched **Modern Wing** at the **Art Institute of Chicago**

Opened in May 2009 as an appendage to the **Art Institute of Chicago**, the Renzo Piano-designed **Modern Wing** highlights modern European art and sculpture, along with contemporary art, photography, architecture, and design from the 20th and 21st centuries. You'll also find renderings by Ludwig Mies van der Rohe and Frank Lloyd Wright. The best way to arrive is via the pedestrian Nichols Bridgeway, which rises from the Millennium Park's Pritzker Great Lawn over the Lurie Gardens. Visit the terrace, where rotating sculpture exhibitions take place, and ever-changing exhibits – including ones for families – offer a precursor to marveling at works by Salvador Dalí, Henri Matisse, Jackson Pollock, and Andy Warhol, to name a few. Museum lectures, gallery talks, and music and dance performances are something else to watch for.

The Art Institute is known as one of the greatest art museums in the world; while you are here, don't forget to see famed works such as Edward Hopper's *Nighthawks*, Georges Seurat's pointillist masterpiece, *A Sunday on La Grande Jatte*, and Grant Wood's *American Gothic*.

Once you've had your fill of iconic art, refuel at anything-but-staid **Terzo Piano**, Tony Mantuano's sunny, stark-white restaurant with an expansive patio and beautiful skyline views. The menu emphasizes what's local, sustainable, and fresh, while local beer and creative cocktail lists are notable as well. Note that the restaurant can be accessed without paying museum admission.

The Art Institute of Chicago; 111 S. Michigan Avenue; tel: 312-443-3600; www.artic.edu; daily 10.30am–5pm, Thur until 8pm; charge, free on first and second Wed of month; map F3
Terzo Piano; 159 E. Monroe Street; tel: 312-443-8650; www.terzopianochicago. com; daily 11am–3pm, Thur also 5–9pm; map F4

Swing with the best of them at **Big City Swing**

Meanwhile, zumba is a more contemporary option for those seeking a dance-cardio workout, and **BYOB Speakeasy Sundays** – held at the **Everleigh Social Club** across the hall – are ideal for anyone who enjoys the dance form, or just prefers to sit back and just enjoy a show. In the event you're uncertain the specific dance style is your cup of tea, you can always watch from the observation deck (advance notice is required). Private lessons are an option, too, for those so inclined.

Big City Swing; 1012 W. Randolph Street; tel: 312-243-0700; www.bigcityswing.com; various times and dates; charge; map A4

Can't get enough of *Dancing with the Stars*? Hightail it to the West Loop's **Big City Swing**, a studio specializing in swing and lindy hop lessons as well as Blues, Balboa, and Charleston instruction. Options range from group classes to private lessons and two-hour, single-session workshops for those not ready to make a full-fledged commitment. On the first Friday of each month, it also hosts a festive BYOB dance at the studio, where DJs play tracks from Count Basie to Benny Goodman, and partners of all skill sets rotate throughout the night. Reservations are not required, and having a partner is not necessary.

A RAUNCHIER OPTION

Starlets in-training can also bust moves at **Studio L'amour** (939 W. Randolph Street, tel: 312-243-6690; studiolamour.com; various times and dates; charge; map A4), a bastion for burlesque bombshells. Presided over by performer Michelle L'amour, this spot welcomes teases-in-training, whatever their level of expertise. Beyond introductory, intermediate and advanced burlesque instruction, participants can learn how to incorporate ballet techniques into routines.

Marvel at the Loop's buildings on a **Chicago Architecture Foundation** tour by train or boat

Chicago's architecture is a sight to behold. Experience it from a different perspective by taking the Chicago Architecture Foundation's **Elevated Architecture: Chicago's Loop by Train** tour, a combined walking and riding trip that also unveils the history of the 'L' transportation system and its impact on surrounding buildings. It's an ideal way to see structures' details, ones that are otherwise missed by pedestrians below. Learn of the significance of the figures appearing on the Hotel Allegro's facade and hear how Trump International Hotel and Tower was made to feel at home within the existing skyline – all from a docent who imparts info through earpieces.

The foundation also offers in-depth neighborhood tours, thematic ones, and lakefront Segway tours that explore the museum campus and Grant Park.

Visitors should also consider cruising on *Chicago's First Lady*, which powers past soaring towers and 50-plus significant sites along the Chicago River, their import revealed by the foundation's knowledgeable guides.

As a more intimate alternative, arrange a two-hour private yacht tour on *Lady Grebe*, a vintage mahogany boat – complete with buffet lunch, cocktails and a tell-all guide – provided you're willing to pay (prices start from $1,550).

Chicago Architecture Foundation; 224 S. Michigan Avenue; tel: 312-922-3432; caf.architecture.org/elevated; various dates at 10.30am; charge; map F3
Chicago's First Lady; Riverside Gardens, Michigan Avenue and Wacker Drive; tel: 847-358-1330; www.cruisechicago. com; Apr 30–Nov 30, Mon–Wed 9am-4pm, Thur–Sun 9am-5.30pm; charge; map F5

Bite into fresh fare from **local farms** at **Chicago's Downtown Farmstand**, then seek out other foodie treats

Eating locally year-round doesn't come without challenges in a city. However, **Chicago's Downtown Farmstand** eases the pain. Stocked with an array of sustainably grown and produced foods, culled from a 250-mile (402km) radius, it's a resource for seasonal, organic vegetables, herbs and fruit, pasture-raised turkey and chicken, naturally sweetened jams, and olive focaccia. Cooking demonstrations and vendor 'trunk shows' allow shoppers to taste produce and shows them how to use what they've procured.

Next, stop by the **Chicago French Market** at the Ogilvie Transportation Center in the West Loop, a permanent, year-round indoor marketplace with about 30 vendor stalls. Popular for its grab-and-go comestibles, it gets flooded with food lovers at lunchtime. Come for the cones of Belgian frites at **Frietkoten** – they're available with a selection of 20 sauces; slather **Fumare Meats'** Montreal-style, smoked pastrami sandwich with spicy mustard; or sink your teeth into a **Saigon Sisters'** *banh mi.* Alternatively, buy macaroons from a World Pastry Champion at **Vanille Patisserie** or some seriously addictive pickles from **Gramp's Gourmet Foods**.

Looking for gifts? You'll also find handmade soaps and fragrant flowers – plus tempting bon bons and truffles – for the taking. There's also live music during lunch.

Another resource for local eats – and fashions – is found at the pop-up **Dose Market** (435 E. Illinois Street; tel: 312-321-1001; map p.01 D1), held monthly in the River East Art Center.

Chicago's Downtown Farmstand; 66 E. Randolph Street; tel: 312-742-8419; www.chicagofarmstand.com; Mon–Fri 11am–7pm, Sat 11am–4pm; map F4 Chicago French Market; 131 N. Clinton Street; tel: 312-575-0306; www. frenchmarketchicago.com; various hours Mon–Sat; map C4

Explore the **underground world** of the **Chicago Pedway**

The bustling, centrally located Loop neighborhood is the site of an under-explored, underground world: the **Chicago Pedway**. Consisting of a network of tunnels, street-level concourses, and bridges that connect storied buildings in the central business district, it runs over 40 city blocks and is nearly five miles in length. Moreover, it's filled with eateries and shops and adorned with public art.

There are multiple points of entry (and exit), including at the **Richard J. Daley Center** (50 W. Washington Street), **Ogilvie Transportation Center** (500 W. Madison Street), and the **Chicago Cultural Center** (78 E. Washington Street). Great for rainy or snowy days, the Pedway is also key to avoiding rush hour traffic. It's also a destination to find **Beard Papa's** fantastic cream puffs (Block 37, 108 N. State Street; tel: 312-960-9000), or you can access lower-level **Marketplace Foods** food court (Macy's, 111 N. State Street; tel: 312-781-1000) if you're seeking sustenance.

There are access points at hotels as well, including **Fairmont Chicago** (200 N. Columbus Drive; tel: 312-565-8000), **Hyatt Regency Chicago** (151 E. Wacker Drive; tel: 312-565-1234), and **Renaissance Chicago Downtown Hotel** (1 W. Wacker Drive; tel: 312-372-7200).

Also of note, the Pedway is linked to the **Art Institute of Chicago** *(p.91)* and the **Harold Washington Library** (400 S. State Street; tel: 312-747-4300). When blazing its trails be prepared, though: it can be a disorienting labyrinth. Fortunately, signage and pavement markings ease at least some of the confusion, as does the detailed map found at www.cityofchicago.org.

Chicago Pedway; 1 W. Randolph Street, with entrances throughout the Loop; www.cityofchicago.org

See **free public art** in the Loop – and understand it, thanks to **Chicago Loop Alliance**

Art lovers will find what fits their fancy in public art in Chicago's Loop. Thanks to the **Chicago Loop Alliance**, locating some of these wonders – and listening to an enlightening audio tour, downloadable to your MP3 player – is as easy as can be. To name but a few, the tour points participants to Chagall's inlaid mosaic *Four Seasons* (Bank One Plaza, West Monroe Street and South Dearborn Street) and *Flamingo* by Alex Calder at Federal Plaza (50 W. Dearborn Street). Keep walking and find Joan Miró's sculpture, *Moon, Sun and One Star (Miss Chicago)* (North Dearborn Street and West Washington Street), Jean Dubuffet's fibreglass *Monument with Standing Beast* at the Helmut Jahn-designed James R. Thompson Center (100 W. Randolph Street); *Untitled* by Picasso at Daley Plaza (Washington and Dearborn streets); and the **Marquette Building** by Holabird & Roche (West Adams Street and South Dearborn Street), where you should head directly to its Dearborn side to see bronze sculptures by Hermon Atkins MacNeil. Also, keep an eye out for the many aesthetic clocks punctuating the streets, including *Father Time* at

35 E. Wacker Drive; the peacock at State and Monroe; and the original Marshall Field's clock, located at Washington and State streets.

The Loop also sees some pop-up art, and it's organized by aptly named **Pop-Up Art Loop**. Work, which can be charted at www.popupartloop.com, appears in vacated storefronts and unexpected public spaces. The organization hosts a **First Thursdays gallery walk,** which is the perfect opportunity to connect with fellow fans. Additional public art is located throughout the city; find it courtesy of the **Chicago Public Art Group** at www.cpag.net.

Various locations in Chicago's Loop; free

Dive into fare from **celebrity chefs** at rock bottom prices at **Macy's**, or catch a **parade**

Located on the seventh floor of **Macy's** department store – the home of erstwhile Marshall Field's – is **Seven on State**, an anything-but-ordinary food court filled with fare from celebrity chefs. Bring your appetite and choose from grass-fed beef, buffalo, and turkey burgers at Marcus Samuelsson's **Marc Burger**; *cochinita pibil* tacos and flatbread-like *huaraches* from Rick Bayless at **Frontera Fresco**; and Takashi Yagihashi's **Noodles by Takashi**, which specializes in brothy bowls of *ramen*. The same floor houses the circa 1907 **Walnut Room**, lined with Circassian walnut-paneled walls and Austrian chandeliers. Its accompanying wine bar, which pours more than 100 selections by the glass, is a fine place to sit for a spell.

Naturally, you'll also want to troll the historic store, a legend listed on the National Register of Historic Places. In addition to stocking everything under the sun – including clothing from Chicago-based designers – the store often features beauty events, book signings and cooking demonstrations. Using Macy's as your base, move on to the shops along **State Street**. Running north-south, it's the site of popular national stores, as well as several restaurants and centrally located hotels. If you happen to be in town during Memorial Day or Thanksgiving weekends, remember that State Street is also home to fantastical parades.

You'll also encounter some nearby on Columbus Drive: the **Puerto Rican parade** in mid-June from Balbo Avenue to Monroe Street is the most buzzed-about event; **Mexican Independence Parade** is also held here in September; and the **St Patrick's Day parade** takes place on this stretch each March. The latter is particularly festive, since the Chicago River is dyed an uncanny shade of green.

Macy's; 7th floor, 111 N. State Street; tel: 312-781-4483; Mon–Thur 10am–8pm, Fri–Sat 8am–10pm, Sun 11am–6pm; map F4

Pass the seasons at **Daley Plaza**, a centrally located epicenter of **events**

Experience Chicago's four seasons by attending midday performances, food-filled ethnic fests, and holiday gatherings at **Daley Plaza**. Situated in the heart of the Loop, this bustling spot is punctuated by Cubist *Untitled*, a renowned steel sculpture by Pablo Picasso. It has appeared in films that include *The Blues Brothers*, *The Fugitive*, and *The Dark Knight*, but its interest extends well beyond the pop-culture-iconic. Spring ushers in the reflective Memorial Day wreath laying ceremony, while the summer means a weekly Thursday farmers' market bountiful with produce and hand-crafted foods. Come October,

'Franken Plaza' goes spooky with aerial circus performances, pyrotechnic shows, and pumpkin decorating. That's also when its fountain is dyed bright orange.

When the holidays arrive, the **Christkindlmarket** pops up. Providing a shopping experience in the German tradition, it's where you can buy unusual ornaments, sip *glühwein* (hot, spiced wine), and snack on rib-sticking sausages and sauerkraut. There's a huge Christmas tree, illuminated with flourish during a post-Thanksgiving ceremony, and appearances by Santa himself. The plaza has also been the site of Asian, Turkish, and Italian festivals among others.

Since it's nearby and ultra-historic, get yourself a seasonal, house-label brew or root beer from **The Berghoff**, along with schnitzel, creamed spinach, and spaetzle. Be sure to pick up a copy of one of the restaurant's cookbooks – they're filled with signature and Berghoff family recipes.

Daley Plaza; Washington and Dearborn streets; tel: 312-744-8524 www.thedaleycenter.com; map E4
The Berghoff; 17 W. Adams Street; tel: 312-427-3170; www.theberghoff.com; Mon–Sat 11am–9pm; map E3

Glean **avant-garde art** from Columbia College Chicago students at the cutting edge **A + D Gallery**

Serving as an exhibition space for both emerging and established artists, the Averill and Bernard Leviton **A+D Gallery** provides a platform for artistic works that range in scope from multimedia visual art to design. Typically, works-in-progress – whether drafts, sketches, or notes – are shown alongside completed pieces to lend insight into the artistic process. Curated by art professionals, the gallery showcases the scope of varied disciplines, which include interior architecture, advertising, and graphic design in addition to fine arts and art history. Keep an eye out for its annual BFA exhibition, which is hung with thought-provoking student work. A + D also hosts a lecture series that delves in-depth into topics like sexual, racial, and gender differences, non-mimetic portraiture, and the impact of one's environment on beliefs.

Columbia College also plays host to **Film Row Cinema** (1104 S. Wabash Avenue; tel: 312-369-6700), the site of screenings and spirited discussions; a **sculpture garden** at the corner of Wabash Avenue and 11th Street; and **The Dance Center** (1306 S. Michigan Avenue; tel: 312-369-8330), which features a choreographic series and classes, workshops and lectures that are open to the public.

Depending on when you visit the campus, you may also encounter improvisational dance performances, destination-worthy exhibits at the **Museum of Contemporary Photography** (600 S. Michigan Avenue; tel: 312-663-5554), or student shows at the **C33 Gallery** (33 E. Congress Parkway; tel: 312-369-6856). Alternatively, there's always the option of attending performances by resident **The Chicago Jazz Ensemble** (Harris Theater for Music and Dance, 205 E. Randolph Street; tel: 312-334-7777).

A + D Gallery; 619 S. Wabash Avenue; tel: 312-369-8687; www.colum.edu/ adgallery; Tue–Sat 11am–5pm, Thur 11am–8pm; map F2

Explore world cuisines, view art, or catch an offbeat show at **Gallery 37 Center for the Arts**

Long synonymous with meat-packing – George W. Dole can be thanked for that – Chicago has a multi-layered food history, taking in successive waves of settlers. The city welcomed New Englanders' 'oyster saloons' in the 1830s and saw foods like corned beef and cabbage popularized in Bridgeport as early as 1836. From German beer and *bratwursts* to Scandinavian *smorgasboards*, and the World's Columbian Exposition of 1893, (which left a legacy of Juicy Fruit gum, Cracker Jack, and shredded wheat) to more recent Chinese and Mexican additions, Chicago's edible history runs deep.

Today, Chicago's multicultural make-up is celebrated at restaurants both celebrated and off the beaten track, and the theme takes center stage at **World Kitchen**, a hands-on, state-of-the-art culinary facility located in **Gallery 37 Center for the Arts**. Specializing in instruction in a wide array of cuisines, topics range from the foods of Chinatown to the flavors of Puglia, Indian sweets and teas, and the makings of Moroccan fare – all taught by industry experts. Single and series classes should be registered for in advance.

Gallery 37 – a family-friendly venue – hosts many other arts programs as well. Spanning five stories, it has its own theater, exhibition space and café. Works from young Chicago artists can be viewed at **CenterSpace Gallery** (tel: 312-744-8925) and at the site's retail store, while **artScape Chicago** (tel: 312-744-9976) features year-round classes for adults, be they photographic in focus or offbeat, like Beijing opera mask-making.

Play-seekers, on the other hand, can settle in at the **Storefront Theater** (tel: 312-742-8497), a showcase for small, Chicago-based performance troupes.

While at the building, be sure to view *Times' Branch*, a mixed media, working clock by Christopher Furman, located in the vestibule; *Moderato Cantabile*, a mosaic relief with totemic and organic shapes, situated in the second floor dance studio and created by Phil Schuster and Mirtes Zwierzynski; and the marquetry *Starring: Labor*, which adorns the theater's marquee and box office window. Created by Jeffrey Goldstein, a fourth-generation Chicago cabinetmaker and carpenter, it's crafted from two-dozen types of wood, among them rare padauk and rosewood from East India.

Before leaving, scope out one-of-a-kind finds in the gift shop, including items made by teens in the endeavor's After School Matters programs. A stop yields everything from funky hand puppets and cookie jars to hats, sculptures, and jewelry boxes.

When you're in this neck of the woods in spring or summer, attend a free show by 'Downtown Sound: New Music Mondays,' a venture from the Chicago Department of Cultural Affairs and the Chicago Office of Tourism. The eclectic

concert series takes place in **Millennium Park** *(p.88)*, which is also the site of the world music-bent Music Without Borders Series, made-in-Chicago jazz acts and experimental music performances.

Gallery 37 Center for the Arts; 66 E. Randolph Street; tel: 312-742-8497; www.chicagoworldkitchen.org, egov. cityofchicago.org/gallery37center; map F4

Pamper yourself at Spa Space, an urban oasis just off the main drag

Everyone needs to be pampered from time to time. That's where **Spa Space** in the West Loop comes in. Nestled into a cozy, serene space, there's nothing cookie cutter about its feel. Specializing in treatments for men, women, and couples, it keeps comfort at the forefront with touches like rain showers, cushy robes, and plush slippers. Following suit, treatments are customized, including its fitness facial, which utilizes a blend of botanical and aromatherapy-based products, and the 'ultraluxe,' said to lift, radiate, and rejuvenate skin to prevent and address signs of aging. Its signature massage combines a variety of disciplines – Swedish, deep tissue, hot stone, Indian head, and aromatherapy. Most pleasingly, its 'head-to-toe' number focuses on the head, body, and – by way of reflexology – feet.

When it comes to body treatments, expect everything from a grapeseed or citrus-herbal body scrub to a detoxifying green tea-ginger-seaweed body wrap. Manicures and pedicures are worthy of mention, too – go for the seasonal variety, which incorporates an aromatic hand scrub and hydrating massage.

Ensuring there's an enjoyable alternative to all-out-healthy spa cuisine, its spa-goers enjoy posh grub from **N9NE Steakhouse**, and gourmet sandwiches and salads come courtesy of indulgent **Pastoral Artisan Cheese, Bread & Wine**. At the end of your sojourn, pick up the house-label shower gel, lotion, shampoo, and conditioner as well as Kobo candles, products from Epicuren, and Vibraderm facial creams for the road.

Spa Space; 161 N. Canal Street; tel: 312-466-9585; Mon 10am–8pm, Tue noon–8pm, Wed–Fri 10am–8pm, Sat 9am–6pm, Sun 11am–5pm; map C4

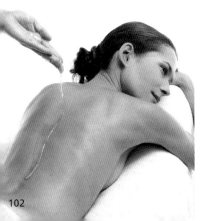

Revel in the **palatial architecture** – plus concerts, films, and dance – at the **Chicago Cultural Center**

Housed in a landmark neo-classical building with beautiful details galore, the **Chicago Cultural Center** is topped by the world's largest Tiffany stained glass dome. It's adorned with ornate details at every turn, including colorful mosaics, molding, and gracious marble. Learn about the building during Wednesday, Friday, and Saturday docent-led tours, which meet in the lobby at 1.15pm.

Beyond the building's lovely looks, there is an inspiring roster of free music, theatre, and dance events that takes place in its surrounds, as well as exhibitions and community and international film screenings. Lectures and discussions often take place, too, and cover subjects such as Chicago bike trails or the city's historic lighthouse. Take in concerts by pianists and violinists, and pause to see plays and movement-based productions.

The first-floor **Chicago Publishers Gallery & Café** is worth a stop; here you'll find a collection of more than 2,300 books and magazines from more than 175 publishers and hundreds of authors based in the Chicago and region. Since it's separated by genres, finding a subject is a cinch.

Also of note is its Project Onward Studio and Jewel Box Gallery, where students with mental and developmental disabilities create one-of-a-kind gifts. If there's one thing you can't leave without seeing, though, it's the **Art-O-Mat** vending machine, found just outside of the main store. Crafted from a recycled cigarette machine, it turns out original works of art for $5 a pop.

Chicago Cultural Center; 78 E. Washington Street; tel: 312-744-6630; www.explorechicago.org; Mon–Thur 8am–7pm, Fri 8am–6pm, Sat 9am–6pm, Sun 10am–6pm; map F4

Map labels:

- West Schubert Avenue
- North Central Park Avenue
- North Kimball Avenue
- North Milwaukee
- Reform Objects
- LOGAN SQUARE
- Wolfbait & B-girls
- Fleur
- West Logan Boulevard
- West Wrightwood Avenue
- N. Sacramento Ave
- West Altgeld Street
- Logan Square
- West Altgeld Stre
- Blue Line
- Avenue
- The Whistler
- West Fullerton Ave
- The Double: An Urban Tavern
- The Burlington
- LOGAN SQUARE
- West Fullerton Avenue
- Cole's
- Dulcelandia Del Sol
- West Belden Avenue
- Revolution Brew
- California
- West Palmer Street
- PALMER SQUARE PARK
- West Dickens Avenue
- North California
- Gal Provocate
- MOZART PARK
- West Armitage Avenue
- West Armitage Avenue
- North Pulaski Avenue
- Weegee's Lounge
- North Lawndale Ave
- North Central Park Avenue
- North Drake Ave
- North Kimball Av nue
- North Spaulding Street
- North Kedzie Avenue
- North Humboldt Boulevard
- West Cortland St
- West
- Armitage
- Avenue
- West Wabansia Avenue
- West Wabansia
- West North Avenue
- West North Avenue
- HUMBOLDT PARK
- HUMBOLDT PARK
- North California Avenue
- Le Moyne Str
- West Hirsch S
- W Potomac Av
- West Division Street

Index listing:

Logan Square, Wicker Park and Ukrainian Village

| 0 | 200 | 400 | 600 | 800 | 1000 yds |
| 0 | 200 | 400 | 600 | 800 | 1000 m |

North Elston Avenue

Kennedy Expressway

Logan Hardware

West Fullerton Avenue

North Elston Avenue

North Western Avenue

HOLSTEIN PARK

G Boutique

90 94

Chicago River North Branch

North Elston Avenue

4

Cat & Mouse Game Store

Margie's Candies

West Armitage Avenue

West Cortland St

North Damen Avenue

North Hoyne Street

BUCKTOWN

North Elston Avenue

Kennedy Expressway

3

North Milwaukee Avenue

Western

L Blue Line

Quimby's Bookstore

The Southern

North

West North Avenue

North Western Avenue

North Avenue

Damen L

Subterranean

Big Star

Double Door
Myopic Books
Reckless Records
Una Mae's Freak Boutique

Ashland Avenue

PULASKI PARK

Goose Island

The Violet Hour

Le Moyne Street

WICKER PARK

WICKER PARK

Wicker Park Landmark District

North Damen Avenue

CLEMENTE PARK

West Division Street

Milk & Honey Café

The Bedford

Division L

Seadog Sushi Bar

West Division St

2

Kstarke Records

West Thomas Street

West Cortez Street

North Hoyne St

Dusty Groove America

Kokorokoko

Labrabbit Optics

Podhalanka

North Milwaukee Avenue

Frontier

Blue Line

North Elston Avenue

West Augusta Boulevard

Club Foot

Mariscos El Veneno

West Augusta Boulevard

Jam

Ukrainian Village Landmark District

Polish Museum of America M

A Vision Chicago

UKRAINIAN

Permanent Records

Dovetail

ECKHART PARK

90

Argentina Leyva Photography

North Western Avenue

West Chicago Avenue

VILLAGE

North Damen Avenue

Very Best Vintage

Sprout Home

West Chicago Avenue

North Ashland Avenue

94

Chicago L

1

West Erie Street

North Ogden Avenue

West Erie Street

Stay within budget on a **vintage shopping spree** in hipster Ukrainian Village and Wicker Park

Within Chicago's Ukrainian Village and Wicker Park neighborhoods you'll find a large concentration of vintage and resale shops stocked with unusual clothing, accessories, and furniture. Rifle through racks at **Dovetail** (1452 W. Chicago Avenue; tel: 312-243-3100), a destination for stylish vintage, mid-century and repurposed duds for modern-minded guys and gals. You may find men's vintage Dior ties, cocktail dresses from eras past, glamorous sunglasses, or rings and necklaces from local line Cities in Dust – not to mention Heywood-Wakefield seating.

Also, watch for art, fashion, and photography events that are hosted on site. Next, make your way to **Very Best Vintage** (1919 W. Chicago Avenue; tel: 312-226-5530), a source for clothing from the 1920s to 1990s. You might be lucky enough to come across a tropical Hawaiian shirt or a punky Betsey Johnson dress. It's also a source for endless kitsch: framed images of Elvis, mod shoe clips, and folksy Scandinavian kitchen tiles. Meanwhile, for back-in-the-day furniture and fashion, **Post 27** (1819 W. Grand Avenue; tel: 312-829–6122) is a must. Turn to it for punchy office armchairs, stylish

directional and mood lighting, and plush silk pillows in addition to beaded 1950s chokers, too-cute journals, and hip prints, all of which can be shipped back home.

Another treasure trove is 1980s and 1990s-bent **Kokorokoko** (1112 N. Ashland Avenue; tel: 773-252-6996), where racks are hung with teal, rhinestone-detailed, brocade-type get-ups and Cross Colors jerseys. Missing that old-school Swatch watch? Find one here, along with local-label attire, including screen-printed t-shirts from Kiyomi Kimble. Be sure to check out the shoes – you'll find a kicking selection of cowboy boots in house. Meanwhile, **Una Mae's Freak Boutique** (1528 N. Milwaukee Avenue; tel: 773-276-7002), as appealing for men as women, proves another key stop for vintage and modern clothing. Even if you come up empty attire-wise, West Third candles and lockets fill the void.

And it's always smart to finish looks with time-warp or modern frames from eyeware shop **Labrabbit Optics** (1104 N. Ashland Avenue; tel: 773-957-4733), marked by a window filled with changing art installations. The collection – bolstered by heavy hitters like Dior and Cazal – also includes frames from Chicago up-and-comer Drift Eyewear.

Because it goes without saying that shopping works up an appetite, you'll need to refuel on potato pancakes at Polish pad **Podhalanka** (1549 W. Division Street; tel: 773-486-6655); Mexican seafood – langostinos in particular – from **Mariscos El Veneno** (1024 N. Ashland Avenue; tel: 773-252-7200); or maki and super white tuna, topped with jalapeno, at **Seadog Sushi Bar** (1500 W. Division Street; tel: 773-235-8100).

Or take your new threads out on the town at **The Bedford** (1612 W. Division Street; tel: 773-235-8800), a restaurant-cum-bar housed in a former bank. It serves updated Midwestern fare and ultra-cool, seasonal cocktails. In the event you seek something more under-the-radar, head to **Club Foot** (1824 W. Augusta Boulevard; tel: 773-489-0379), a toy and memorabilia-filled Ukie Village dive bar with DJ-spun tunes, a pool table, and dirt-cheap drink specials. When the hours wane, keep a watch for the 'Tamale Guy,' who often makes a late-night appearance to the joy of hungry revelers.

Ukrainian Village and Wicker Park;
map p.106–107

Unearth **literary treasures** at three-story **Myopic Books**

Mind the rules at musty Wicker Park stalwart, **Myopic Books**: be sure to turn off your cell phone ringer, and return what you've looked at to its rightful place. The decades-old reseller – a fixture long before it was hip to be square – warrants a visit for both the casual reader and niche enthusiast. Browse its three rambling, maze-like floors towering with over 80,000 editions. Housing endless genres, ranging from sci-fi to cooking, biography, literary criticism, and children's lit, it also features books of local interest, which is just the thing for those wanting to acquaint themselves with the city.

The shop also has a selection of new, collectible, and rare titles.

While you're exploring the shelves, keep in mind that the store hosts an ongoing experimental music series on Monday evenings – the longest running of its kind – along with semi-weekly readings and talks from poets. Come on Tuesdays, and see the Wicker Park Chess Club at work on its second floor – and join in, whatever your skill level, free of charge. Also of note, the nook buys quality books during designated hours – a good way to unload plane reads.

If you're specifically seeking indie magazines, comics, or graphic novels – make fast tracks to the equally lauded **Quimby's Bookstore** on North Avenue. The shop recently launched its own podcast series; recorded live at the store, it features musings by authors of note. Quimby's also often hosts literary events.

Myopic Books; 1564 N. Milwaukee Avenue; tel: 773-862-4882; www.myopicbookstore.com; daily 9am–11pm; map F3
Quimby's Bookstore; 1854 W. North Avenue; tel: 773-342-0910; www.quimbys.com; Mon–Thur noon–9pm, Fri noon–10pm, Sat 11am–10pm, Sun noon–7pm; map F3

Return to **another era** at pre-Prohibition-inspired
The Violet Hour, or craft your own libations

Classic cocktails are all the rage, and there are few better places to find them than at Wicker Park's Victorian-feeling drinking parlor, **The Violet Hour**. Hung with curtains and trimmed with crown molding, refined, high-backed seating, and twinkly chandeliers, it's nonetheless the cocktails – and the bartenders who make them – that command the stage. Libations are seasonal but may include the amour-inducing Juliet and Romeo, with Beefeater gin, mint, cucumber, and rose water. Prefer something with a bit more zip? Try the Barbed Wire Daisy, a mixture of Weller 107, lemon, house grenadine, and Saigon cinnamon syrup.

Since patrons tend to linger, making seating limited, it's good to know there are plenty of other places pouring expert throwback cocktails nearby. Try **Weegee's Lounge** in Logan Square, for classic creations and a solid beer selection. Exuding casual charm, it's lined with off-kilter black and white crime scene photos and emanates with conversation-friendly jazz and blues tunes. Settle in and order a Manhattan, take pics in the photo booth, or challenge mates to a game of shuffleboard.

If cocktails are really your thing, why not learn to make perfect ones firsthand? Sign up for a workshop with mixology master Paul McGee at **The Whistler**. Part art gallery, record label, and live music venue, the lounge also provides intimate, hands-on instruction, along with a handful of house recipes.

The Violet Hour; 1520 N. Damen Avenue; tel: 773-252-1500; www. theviolethour.com; Sun-Fri 6pm-2am, Sat 6pm-3am; map F3
Weegee's Lounge; 3659 W. Armitage Avenue; tel: 773-384-0707; daily 5pm-2am; map B4
The Whistler; 2421 N. Milwaukee Avenue; tel: 773-227-3530; www. whistlerchicago.com; Mon-Thur 6pm-2am, Fri, Sun 5pm-2am, Sat 5pm-3am; map C5

Treat little ones to whimsical **Mexican candy** from **Dulcelandia Del Sol**, then play some games

in Bucktown. Specializing in unplugged entertainment for all ages, you'll find little-known strategy games in addition to family, card, and board games; disentanglement and visual-spatial puzzles; and cubes that cause conundrums (and some under-the-breath cursing). Naturally, you'll find all the classics, too, including dominos, casino ready card-shufflers, and backgammon in a dizzying array of fancy cases, including walnut, lizard, and burlwood varieties.

Whether you call it saccharine central or a dentist's worst nightmare, one thing is for sure: you'll feel like a kid in a candy shop at **Dulcelandia Del Sol**. Featuring the area's best selection of marshmallow bonbons, *dulce de leche* candies, and gummies, it has plenty of unusual spicy (tamarind-chili) and regular (cherry) lollipops as well. This whimsical sugar shack also stocks all the necessities for parties, including piñatas that beg to be filled, balloons, games, streamers, and character-driven favors. Come Halloween, the Mexican festival of Day of the Dead, or the holiday season, it's also a must for seasonal confections.

Since a youthful tone has already been set, explore more than 600 mind-bending games at **Cat & Mouse Game Store**

The best time to give the place a whirl, though, is on Tuesdays at 6.30pm, when it hosts family game night. Then, patrons can play games from its collection or tackle ones they've brought from home. The store also hosts a monthly club for yo-yo enthusiasts. Ask in advance about preview parties for new games as well.

Dulcelandia Del Sol; 3855 W. Fullerton Avenue; tel: 773-235-7825; www. dulcelandia.com; Sat 9am-7pm, Apr-Oct Sun-Fri 10am-8pm, Nov-Mar Sun-Fri 10am-7pm; map A5
Cat & Mouse Game Store; 2212 W. Armitage Avenue; tel: 773-384-4454; www.cat-n-mouse.com; Tue 10am-10pm, Wed 10am-8pm, Thur-Sat 10am-7pm, Sun 11am-5pm; map E4

Grab tickets to a **live show** at bi-level club, **Double Door**

Wicker Park has a bevy of hipster haunts, and Joe Shanahan's **Double Door** nightclub – poised at the neighborhood's iconic six-corner intersection – is one of its staples. Its name nods to the fact that it has two entrances, though only the Damen one is used by non-musicians. Once you've made it past the bouncers and paid the cover, you'll be greeted by a super-dark, dive-y space, with a nude muralled-bar. Venerable enough to host the Rolling Stones and Smashing Pumpkins (sometimes under pseudonyms) over the years, it's small enough to feel personal.

Mostly, rock bands are the focus – though line-ups from hip-hop to new country certainly appear and take the elevated stage in plain view. Downstairs, there's a small bar and pool tables with screens tuned to the show above. Movie buffs will also appreciate the place, given parts of *High Fidelity* were filmed here.

After the gig, check out the nightlife scene along North and Milwaukee avenues, where you'll find live concert venue **Subterranean** (2011 W. North Avenue; tel: 773-278-6600; map F3), a hotbed for indie acts and **The Southern** (1840 W. North Avenue; tel: 773-342-1840; map F3), known for its regional American fare and funky cocktails, while Paul Kahan's honky tonk taqueria and whiskey bar, **Big Star** (1531 N. Damen Avenue; tel: 773-235-4039; map F3) is only a stone's throw away.

Double Door; 1551 N. Damen Avenue; tel: 773-489-3160; www.doubledoor.com; various times and prices; map F3

Keep your eyes peeled for avant-garde exhibits at **Gallery Provocateur** or shop for your own exhibition

Exhibition and performance venue **Gallery Provocateur** is the brainchild of Veronika Kotljaic, ex-curator of the defunct, erotic Echo Gallery. Showcasing four annual shows, often themed, this not-for-profit spot presents figurative, fantasy work from local and international artists, hanging them in an intimate, multi-room space set within the historic, domed Congress Theatre. See everything from limited edition, signed lithographs to acrylics on board. The place sometimes teams with likeminded groups, like Naked Girls Reading (nakedgirlsreading. com), a women's book club whose members unapologetically read clothes-free. Come for cocktail receptions, too, usually hosted when new shows are launched.

Leave the kiddos at home and learn more about things that inspire such work – if you dare – at Edgewater's **Leather Archives and Museum** (6418 N. Greenview Avenue; tel: 773-761-9200; p.44 map B8), a showcase for erotic prints, archival papers, and records and collateral from clubs. It's also where you can eye leather attire and boots with historic significance, plus periodicals and photography for those of a certain persuasion. The museum also features eight exhibit galleries and has a short film screening room.

For something more lasting, exhibitionists might book a boudoir session at **Argentina Leyva Photography** (764 N. Milwaukee Avenue, tel: 630-667-4633; map H1). In preparation, you'll need underthings, so pop into **G Boutique** (2131 N. Damen Avenue; tel: 773-235-1234; map F4), which provides pin up workshops. Otherwise, go to Lincoln Park's ultra-classy **Isabella Fine Lingerie** (840 W. Armitage Avenue; tel: 773-281-2352; map p.44 C3).

Gallery Provocateur; 2125 N. Rockwell Street; tel: 773-661-2341; galleryprovocateur.org; by appointment and various hours when exhibits are scheduled; map D4

Discover strange plants at **Sprout Home**, then pick up a romantic bouquet from **Fleur**

Upon stepping into **Sprout Home**, you'll have entered a wonderfully weird, moss-cloaked fairyland, one filled with unique plants – tillandsia, in particular – tucked into modern pots and odd vessels, hung from the ceiling, and nestled into nooks along with terrariums, statuary, and candles. Located along a less-traveled stretch of Damen Avenue, it's filled with functional decorative items, many local and some of them eco-minded. It's also a resource for centerpiece-worthy serving dishes. But don't stop there: Sprout's outdoor garden is a jungle of passion flowers, wild, ornamental grasses, and organic veggies and herbs. Wander through the looming foliage, making your way up to its sleek rooftop deck, which is stacked with planters and pots, for further inspiration.

On the other hand, if cut flowers are your forte, you should grab an exotic bouquet – one that spells romance – at **Fleur** in Logan Square. Recognized for its modern-meets-woodsy approach – asymmetrical blue, gray, and yellow arrangements with sprigs of dusty miller, billy balls, and succulents, for example – the shop also sells items from local producers, including handmade soaps, fragrant bath products, gifts for babies, and candles.

If you're in a shopping state of mind, continue the affair at **Wolfbait & B-girls** (3131 W. Logan Boulevard; tel: 312-698-8685; map C5), a women's clothing boutique with in-house collections and local labels, or visit **Reform Objects** (2620 N. Milwaukee Avenue; tel: 312-350-5604; map C5), a spot to score Mid-Century modern furniture and covetable home accessories.

Sprout Home; 745 N. Damen Avenue; tel: 312-226-5950; sprouthome.stores. yahoo.net; Mon-Fri 9am-8pm, Sat-Sun 9am-7pm; map F1
Fleur; 3149 W. Logan Boulevard; tel: 773-395-2770; www.fleurchicago.com; Tue-Fri 10am-7pm, Sat 10am-5pm, Sun noon-4pm; map C5

Roll out of bed to munch **contemporary brunch** at **Jam**

Located in the hip Ukrainian Village, **Jam** turns out modern, affordable brunch with special occasion appeal. It's not surprising, really, given a veteran of Charlie Trotter's and North Pond is in the kitchen, whipping up a pork cheek and egg sandwich with green apple ketchup; cured trout quiche with fried capers and bagel chip panzanella; and malted custard French toast. But later sleepers need not fret since choices are enticing as the day wears on.

Cases in point are the Butterkase-topped burger with smoked tomato sauce and seared escolar, or butterfish, with pineapple gnocchi and pear emulsion. The only question is where to enjoy it: in the cheery, sophisticated dining room, punctuated by plexi-glass chairs, or the tree-shaded garden patio, perfect on a sunny morning.

If you are planning a hair of-the-dog visit, plan to BYO, grabbing a bottle from nearby **A Vision Chicago** (910 N. Damen Avenue; tel: 773-227-5700; map F1), a recommended flower and wine boutique. Whatever you do, remember to bring cash since credit cards are not accepted at the restaurant. And do be on the watch for the occasional midnight 'brunch', the perfect place to visit after an evening hitting bars.

When seating is scarce, you won't be disappointed with the alternative of **Milk & Honey Café** (1920 W. Division Street; tel: 773-395-9434; map F2), beloved for its house granola. Be sure to try Rick Bayless's Mexican Mix with roasted pumpkin seeds, peanuts, and cacao nibs.

Jam; 937 N. Damen Avenue; tel: 773-489-0302; www.jamrestaurant.com; Wed–Mon 7am–3pm; map F2

Browse for new and used tunes – on both CD and vinyl – at **Reckless Records**

A mainstay for indie rock and tunes from local bands, new and used music store **Reckless Records** is on a short-list among local music geeks. Flip through the vast selection, organized by sub-genres, like Kraut/Prog/Psychedelic, or Trip-Hop. Then take to its listening stations to ensure you've made the right pick. Staffers tag albums deemed worthy with write-ups, offering listeners pre-approval of sorts. In addition to selling CDs and graded vinyl, the shop additionally stocks DVDs, VHS movies, and video games as well as a selection of underground magazines. Sometimes the site of intimate, in-store performances, it also welcomes the occasional listening party for like-minded enthusiasts. Also, watch for employees' year-end, best-of lists, and consider buying online when you're not in town. The

OTHER GREAT RECORD STORES
Continue your music-buying spree at other area greats, perhaps **Permanent Records** (1914 W. Chicago Avenue; tel: 773-278-1744; map F1), **Logan Hardware** (2410 W. Fullerton Avenue; tel: 773-235-5030; map E5), or **Kstarke Records** (1109 N. Western Avenue; tel: 773-772-4880; map E2). Another quintessential spot is **Dusty Groove America** (1120 N. Ashland Avenue; tel: 773-342-5800; map G2). Revered for its rare and imported soul, jazz, lounge, Brazilian, and hip-hop selection, it also sells turntables and equipment to DJs-in-waiting. In addition to having a prolific online store, Dusty Groove has an eponymous, adjunct record label, which carries sought-after, out-of-print albums, which it reissues on CD.

website's inventory, which includes everything available at Reckless's three Chicago locations, is updated every 24 hours.

Reckless Records; 1532 N. Milwaukee Avenue, tel: 773-235-3727; www.reckless. com; Mon–Sat 10am–10pm, Sun 10am–8pm; map F3

117

Chuckle at a **comedic open mic night** or catch a live performance at **Cole's**

A tavern at heart, **Cole's** is a no-frills, Logan Square hangout from former accountant and musician Coleman Brice. Strung with work from local artists, it houses a prominent stage, where bands – ranging in genre from rockabilly to punk and rock – play for free most nights of the week. The beer selection goes beyond what's ordinary, so don't be surprised to find Two Brothers Domaine DuPage French Country Ale or a nitro tap of Old # 38 Stout. But the real fun begins on Wednesday nights at 9.30pm when comedic variety band Foz the Hook kicks off a hosted, humorous open mic night; come early if you want to get involved firsthand, though, since signup starts at 7pm.

After laughing it up, proceed to wood-paneled, antler-hung lair **The Burlington** (3425 W. Fullerton Avenue; tel: 773-384-3243; map B5). Exuding the vibe of an old man joint, it's also the site of DJ-fueled dance parties, candlelit tables, and a jovial beer-swilling clientele. The last Sunday of each month, The Burlington also hosts a sex-themed show with a love life quandary-solving Q&A session, plus sultry readings by local writers and trivia games that result in prize-winning.

When the place gets packed, as it often does, make your way to **The Double: An Urban Tavern** (3545 W. Fullerton Avenue; tel: 773-772-7000; map B5), a casual, pretension-free tap with a smart selection of craft beer and eclectic music on an old-timey juke. En route, treat yourself to a hot fudge-drizzled sundae from **Margie's Candies** (1960 N. Western Avenue; 773-384-1035; map E4), which stays open until midnight each night.

Cole's; 2338 N. Milwaukee Avenue; tel: 773-276-5802; www.coleschicago.com; Mon–Fri 5.30pm–2am, Sat 3.30pm–3am, Sun 4pm–2am; map C5

Tip back some of the changing rotation craft drafts at **Revolution Brewing**

A tin ceiling and repurposed lighting, made from Goose Island Bourbon County Stout barrels, set the tone at Josh Deth's **Revolution Brewing**, where Jim Cibak crafts nearly three-dozen house-made beers throughout the year. Not surprisingly, the duo goes way back: they met at the Goose Island facility in the 1990s. Peer through the window in the rear to see where the magic happens. Or for an insider's look, arrive on Saturdays at noon to tour its brewery – if you're 21 and over, that is. Although a 'no reservation' policy can mean tables are hard to come by, pints of coriander and orange peel-spiked Bottom Up Wit or malty, chocolatey Eugene will make you quick to forgive.

Whether you follow with a tulip glass filled with Coup d'Etat, a dry-hopped, spicy French-style saison, or a pint of toasty Repo Man Rye Stout, it's safe to assume bites like bacon fat popcorn; hard cider-steamed mussels with blue cheese and Granny Smith apples; and pizzas turned from a hearth-style oven are perfect foils.

There are a handful of other local, small-batch brewpubs in Chicago that are also worth checking out, including **Half Acre Beer Company** (4257 N. Lincoln Avenue; tel: 773-248-4038; map p.25 A4), **Metropolitan Brewing** (5121 N. Ravenswood Avenue; www.metrobrewing.com; map p.24 B5) and wood-swathed **Haymarket Pub & Brewery** (737 W. Randolph Street; tel: 312-638-0700; p.86 map B5).

Revolution Brewing; 2323 N. Milwaukee Avenue; tel: 773-227-2739; revbrew.com; Mon-Fri 11am-2am, Sat-Sun 10am-2am; map D4

South Loop, Little Italy, Chinatown, and Pilsen

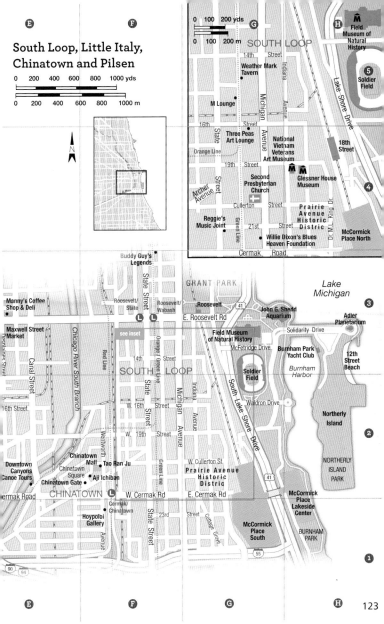

South Loop, Little Italy, Chinatown and Pilsen

SOUTH LOOP

Field Museum of Natural History

5 Soldier Field

14th Street

Weather Mark Tavern

M Lounge

16th Street

Three Peas Art Lounge

National Vietnam Veterans Art Museum

18th Street

Orange Line

19th Street

Second Presbyterian Church

Glessner House Museum

4

Cullerton Street

Archer Avenue

Prairie Avenue Historic Distric

Reggie's Music Joint

21st Street

McCormick Place North

Green Line

Willie Dixon's Blues Heaven Foundation

Cermak Road

Buddy Guy's Legends

GRANT PARK

Lake Michigan

3

Manny's Coffee Shop & Deli

Roosevelt/ State

Roosevelt/ Wabash

Roosevelt

E. Roosevelt Rd

John G. Shedd Aquarium

Adler Planetarium

Maxwell Street Market

see inset

Field Museum of Natural History

Solidarity Drive

Canal Street

Chicago River South Branch

Red Line

14th Street

McFetridge Drive

Burnham Park Yacht Club

12th Street Beach

SOUTH LOOP

Orange/ Green Line

Soldier Field

Burnham Harbor

16th Street

W. 16th Street

Waldron Drive

Northerly Island

2

Downtown Canyons Canoe Tours

Chinatown Mall

Tao Ran Ju

W. 19th Street

NORTHERLY ISLAND PARK

Chinatown Square

Aji Ichiban

W. Cullerton St.

Chinatown Gate

W. Cermak Rd

Prairie Avenue Historic Distric

E. Cermak Rd

CHINATOWN

Cermak/ Chinatown

McCormick Place Lakeside Center

McCormick Place South

BURNHAM PARK

Hoypoloi Gallery

23rd Street

Cottage Grove

1

90 94

Wentworth Avenue

State Street

55

E F G H

123

Spend the day at the **Museum Campus** on the shores of Lake Michigan

The location of several of Chicago's most esteemed museums and 91-acre (37-hectare) Northerly Island, the South Loop's **Museum Campus** is the perfect place to while away a day. Created when Lake Shore Drive was rerouted in 1998, it's where you'll find the **Field Museum** (1400 S. Lake Shore Drive; tel: 312-922-9410). Named for its benefactor, Marshall Field, it houses over 21 million specimens, among them artifacts from ancient Egypt, taxidermy African elephants, and a large, impressive dinosaur collection. The real star of the show, however, is Sue, the world's largest and most complete Tyrannosaurus Rex.

From there, it's just a short jaunt to the **John G. Shedd Aquarium** (1200 S. Lake Shore Drive; tel: 312-939-2438), where you can escape to a Caribbean reef, see a flooded Amazonian forest, and explore the waters of the world and the aquatic life that lives within. Watch for its oldest resident, Granddad, an Australian lungfish who's been strutting his stuff since 1933. And be sure to catch the reef dive and the aquatic show put on by resident dolphins and beluga whales. Visitors can also book a behind-the-scenes tour to see how animals are cared for, become a marine mammal trainer for a day, or arrange to participate in a penguin encounter. Sometimes, there are even in-house sleepovers.

Meanwhile, space enthusiasts will dig the **Adler Planetarium** (1300 S. Lake Shore Drive; tel: 312-922-7827), which

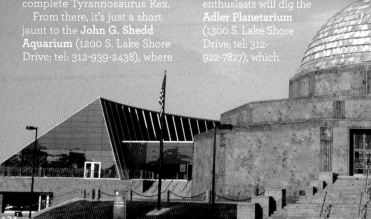

houses the interactive Planet Explorers exhibit for young ones, not to mention viewing of fully restored Gemini 12 spacecraft. On the third Thursday of every month, it also hosts Adler After Dark, a 21-plus cocktail soiree, during which time you can peer through the observatory's telescope to see Saturn's rings at night.

Just to the south of the planetarium, visit the Daniel H. Burnham–designed peninsula, **Northerly Island** (1400 S. Lynn White Drive; tel: 312-742-7529), which – along with Burnham Park – was selected as the location of Chicago's second World's Fair in 1933–4. Today, you'll encounter rambling walking paths flanked with wild grasses, ample skyline views, and some of the city's best fishing. It's also the site of a 7,500-seat concert venue, where popular artists perform and family-friendly festivities are often scheduled. Additionally, it's where seasonal sailing lessons launch for those aged 18 and up.

Not to be ignored is the **12th Street Beach** (1200 S. Lake Shore Drive; tel: 312-742-7529), along with a nature center and bird sanctuary and hospital. Meanwhile, to the east of the island is **Soldier Field** (1410 S. Museum Campus Drive; tel: 312-235-7000), home of the Chicago Bears. During the off-season, it hosts other events, including concerts and Chicago Fire soccer games. Tours of the stadium – which include stops at a skyline suite and inside the visitors' locker room – can also be arranged.

Southeast corner of Grant Park, Lake Shore Drive; map G3–H2

Get **communal** at Chinatown's **Tao Ran Ju**, a sleek spot for hot pots and xiao long bao

Chinatown is one of the city's most distinctive neighborhoods, with architecture that is reason enough for a trip, including the Nine Dragon Wall, Cermak and Wentworth's iconic Chinatown Gate. But really, it's the endless array of enticing eats that most people come for. Daters and groups alike favor **Tao Ran Ju**, a BYO hot pot spot. Located within Chinatown Mall, its marble-topped tables are outfitted with high-tech induction burners at each seat, so everyone – whatever their persuasion – can have things their way. Start by picking a broth base; the spicy version,

when bolstered by pickled daikon, chilis, and peppercorns, packs a particular punch. But less adventuresome types can seek comfort in the miso or earthy mushroom varieties.

From there, it's time to add a few types of veg – maybe chrysanthemum greens or golden needle mushrooms – followed by meat and seafood, such as sliced lamb, wisps of beef, and scallops. There are more challenging options, too, like goose intestines and duck tongue. Finally, you'll want to tack on some noodles and customize your creation with condiments, such as garlic and toasted sesame chilis. Don't forget grab sauces as well, like *sha cha* or chive flower, which are key for dunking ingredients.

Since not everyone gets into the DIY approach, it's handy to know the kitchen's fiery *niu rou mian* (beef noodle soup) is a satisfying – and house-prepared – alternative. Save room for the pork or crab roe *xiao long bao* (soup dumplings) and the nicely spiced lamb skewers as well.

Tao Ran Ju; 2002 S. Wentworth Avenue; tel: 312-808-1111; daily 10.30am–1am; map F2

Absorb the complexity and kaleidoscopic colors at
The National Museum of Mexican Art

Pilsen was originally populated by immigrants from Germany, Ireland, and later, the Czech Republic and Poland, though today it's largely a thriving Mexican-American community – a fact that's apparent when you're walking along its 18th Street commercial corridor. It's filled with bakeries, *taquerias*, and grocers with a distinctly south of the border feel.

Throughout the neighborhood, iconographic, spirited murals can be found. Look for standouts at the **Cooper Dual Language Academy** (2100 S. Damen Avenue), at **1900 S. Ashland Avenue**, and at the **18th Street Pink Line Station** (1645 W. 18th Street). After viewing the murals, move on to see more at the **National Museum of Mexican Art**, a decades-old cultural center loaded with historic Mexican-American artwork. Its collection of over 6,000 objects – including pre-Cuauhtémoc ceramics – gives way to a researcher's dream: more than 2,400 works on paper. It's also a place to see dance dresses and weavings, masks for Day of the Dead (a Mexican holiday honoring the memories of departed loved ones), and figurines and photography of 19th-century Mexico. The museum offers educational programming as well, including film and literature events, culinary gatherings, and dance and theatrical performances. Not to be forgotten, an on-site store features work by Mexican and Mexican-American artists.

Pilsen is also the location of the **Chicago Arts District** (1915 S. Halsted Street; tel: 312-738-8000; map D2), several blocks of loft-like galleries, studios and retail spaces. Come, if you can, on the second Friday of the month, when more than 30 galleries open to the public. Or pay a visit anytime to **St Paul Catholic Church** (2127 W. 22nd Place; tel: 773-847-7622; map A1), a 1903 structure built without a single nail.

National Museum of Mexican Art; 1852 W. 19th Street; tel: 312-738-1503; www. nationalmuseumofmexicanart.org; Tue–Sun 10am–5pm; free; map B2

Soak up the city from the water on a **canoe tour**

The outfit also hosts a 'Chicago River Wilderness' ride through Lake and Cook counties to see herons, turtles, frogs, minks, and deer in their natural climes. There's also a peaceful, moonlit lagoon adventure in 'North Suburban Skokie' on offer, complete with campfire cooking. Those trips make it possible for most ages and skill levels to see the city by boat.

Another outfit to try is **Chicago River Canoe and Kayak**, which also launches from the city. Participants can enjoy moonlight dinner paddles, with a riverside picnic. Meanwhile, 'Skyscraper Canyon' excursions ply past River City, the Willis Tower, Opera House, and forks of the river in canoes or tandem kayaks. Guided rambles to dam lagoons and combined pedals and paddles are options as well. Chicago River Canoe and Kayak also simply offers lessons and rents canoes.

Walking tours can be interesting, but they don't hold a candle to a canoe adventure with **Downtown Canyons Canoe Tours**. The group, as its name implies, organizes urban explorations by boat. A bus brings participants to the Lake Shore Drive bridge house to start the leisurely float. Dry bags and flotation devices are provided, and there's a lesson in paddling preparedness and a bit of equipment familiarization. Then from the east end of the main stem of the Chicago River, paddlers travel west to Wolf Point, north to Goose Island, and south toward River City.

Downtown Canyons Canoe Tours; from Lawrence Fisheries, 2120 S. Canal Street; tel: 312-939-0490; chicagoriver. org/paddle; charge; map E2
Chicago River Canoe and Kayak; 3400 N. Rockwell Street; tel: 773-704-2663; chicagoriverpaddle.com; charge; p.25 map A2

Sip locally produced **Metropolis Coffee** and funky cocktails, while seeing art at **Three Peas Art Lounge**

There's nothing intimidating about the gallery experience at the South Loop's **Three Peas Art Lounge**, a storefront-style exhibition space that also dispenses an extensive selection of libations and steaming, bottomless mugs of local Metropolis coffee. Owners also created their own line of wines with grapes that come from Washington State and are produced and blended at Von Stiehl Winery in Wisconsin. The bottles' labels, signed by and branded with artists' biographies, include Riesling and Cabernet Sauvignon varieties. They can be enjoyed in flights, along with non-house selections, or by the eight-or-11-ounce pour. Martini flights are an option as well. Try one with a red velvet cupcake or posh pastry at the intimate, stool-lined bar.

The venue's real thrust, however, is its visual art – primarily paintings, photography, and pottery – hailing from emerging artists. Take your time to appreciate them, and watch for occasional networking events and workshops, aimed at bringing knowledge of disciplines down to earth. Afterward, you might stop at **Hoypoloi Gallery** (2235 S. Wentworth Avenue; tel: 312-225-6477; map F1), a spot for artsy

object shopping, from housewares to home furnishings. And, since Three Peas is not open especially late, think about having a nightcap at live venue **Reggie's Music Joint** (2105 S. State Street; tel: 312-949-0120; map G4); jazzy **M Lounge** (1520 S. Wabash Avenue; tel: 312-447-0201; map G5); or **Weather Mark Tavern** (1503 S. Michigan Avenue; tel: 312-588-0230; map G5), a casual, nautical watering hole serving sea-inspired beverages, like Pirate's Punch with Mount Gay rum and cranberry and orange juices.

Three Peas Art Lounge; 75 E. 16th Street; tel: 312-624-9414; www.threepeasartlounge.com; Mon–Sat 5–11pm; map G4

Find everything under the sun – and **Mexican street food** – at the **Maxwell Street Market**

Significant enough to inspire a documentary and extensive written documentation on its food vendors, **Maxwell Street Market** is part of the fiber of Chicago. The original gathering was held on its namesake thoroughfare, from Halsted Street to 16th Street and began in the 1800s as a haven for European immigrants. It grew to become an impressive open-air market, where things both legal and not-so-legal were sold. Much of it, from clothes to auto parts and appliances, was allegedly stolen from railcars and hawked at bargain basement prices. (This, despite its proximity to the former Chicago Police Academy.) Dubbed the 'Ellis Island of the Midwest,' it proved a multicultural phenomenon, selling wares from Asia to Mexico. To the chagrin of locals, in 1994, the market was moved to Canal Street due to University of Illinois at Chicago expansion. It was again relocated in September 2008.

Over the years, the market gave rise to the indigenous Maxwell Street Polish sandwich – a fried or grilled sausage finished with yellow mustard and topped with grilled onions and sport peppers. If you're interested in a taste, try it around the clock at

Jim's Original (1250 S. Union Avenue; tel: 312-733-7820) or **Express Grill Original Maxwell St Polish** (1260 S. Union Avenue; tel: 312-738-2112). But bear in mind, it's the Mexican street food served at the market that's most deserving of accolades. Wander its east and west aisles on Sundays year-round, searching for Oaxacan *tamales* steamed in banana leaves; sauce drenched *tortas ahogadas* ('pambazos') topped with pickled onions; and *huarache*, griddled masa discs crowned with steak. You'll also encounter less commonly consumed fare, like offal and eyeball tacos and sippable *consommé de chivo* (goat broth). From there, it's on to tacos in hand-hewn tortillas from Rubi's; *elotes*, lime-spritzed corn topped with dry cheese, mayo, and chili powder; and *pupusas*, flat cornmeal pancakes stuffed with cheese and finished with pickled cabbage. But that's not to say the zucchini flower-stuffed quesadillas aren't worth your time. Ditto the churros – especially when they're being served freshly fried.

While you're wandering the bazaar, also take notice of the produce, which ranges from fuchsia-hued hibiscus leaf to *nopales* and tamarind pods. You might even encounter an event, maybe a Double Dutch contest, on your travels.

Before coming, learn of the market's history by watching Phil Ranstrom's *Cheat You Fair: The Story of Maxwell Street*, which showed at the Sundance Film Festival. It chronicles not only the history of Maxwell Street Market, but also the development of electrified, urban blues ('Chicago Blues') on Maxwell Street and the fight that ensued to save the market

from ruin. Since you're so close to another Chicago legend, finish your day at **Manny's Coffee Shop & Deli** (1141 S. Jefferson Street; tel: 312-939-2855), a singular spot for corned beef sandwiches, matzo ball soup, and crisp potato pancakes dolloped with apple sauce. Other rib-sticking options – favored by the cops and politicos – range from oxtail stew to blintzes and apple slices.

Maxwell Street Market; Des Plaines Street and Roosevelt Road; tel: 312-745-4676; www.maxwellstreetmarket.us; Sun 7am–3pm; free; map E3

Get a modern-day taste of **Little Italy**

Mason jars filled with spreadable goodness team with ragout-topped polenta boards, salumi and quartinos of wine at chill **Davanti Enoteca** (1359 W. Taylor Street; tel: 312-226-5550), a Little Italy haunt that's helping to lead the Old-World neighborhood's present-day renaissance. The rustic dining room, done up in exposed brick and repurposed wood, also offers daily specials, a nice selection of pasta, and antipasti poised for sharing.

This neck of the woods offers rich pickings for tasty Italian bites (*see box, below*), but wherever you indulge, skip the tiramisu and wander over to seasonal, family-run stand, **Mario's Italian Lemonade** (1068 W. Taylor Street; tel: 312-829-0672). Only open in the summer, it serves something quintessentially Chicago: fruit-flavored ice.

Since Little Italy is about more than just edibles, be sure to add on a visit to the **National Italian American Sports Hall of Fame** (1431 W. Taylor Street; tel: 312-226 5566) or the ornate, French Romanesque **Notre Dame de Chicago** (1335 W. Harrison Street; tel: 312-243-7400). You will spot its dome from a distance; inside, find the interior swathed in stained glass, marble and hues of blue and gold.

Little Italy; map C3–D3

> ### CLASSIC ITALIAN SPOTS
> Little Italy is, unsurprisingly, the place for fans of traditional Italian fare to get their fix: red sauce options are still prevalent in town. Winners include **Rosal's** (1154 W. Taylor Street; tel: 312-243-2357), **Bacchanalia** (2413 S Oakley Avenue; tel: 773-254-6555), and **Tuscany** (1014 W. Taylor Street; tel: 312-829-1990). Alternatively, if great subs are your thing, just stop by **Conte Di Savoia** (1438 W Taylor Street; tel: 773-666-3471) or Fontano Foods (1058 W. Polk Street; tel: 312-421-4474) for a simple but sublime sandwich.

Get a case of the **blues** at **Willie Dixon's Blues Heaven Foundation**

Chicago's history with blues music runs deep – it emerged in the 1920s during the Great Migration. Among the first artists to record locally were Alberta Hunter and Cow Cow (Charles) Davenport for Paramount Records. Later, other musicians like Georgia Tom brought gospel music to the modern day, and artists, including Big Bill (William), performed on the city's South Side.

Experience a slice of this history at the former Chess Records Office and Studios, now **Willie Dixon's Blues Heaven Foundation** in the South Loop. Among the icons to have recorded there are the Rolling Stones, whose instrumental *2120 S. Michigan Avenue* canonized the address. In 1993, the landmark building was bought by Dixon's widow, Marie.

Now, tours show off the wood-paneled offices of Leonard and Phil Chess and the shipping and receiving rooms. Upstairs, you'll also see the rehearsal room, main studio, and control room. Additionally, the joint hosts a bi-monthly series focusing on individuals who helped shape the blues, while featuring music nights in the studio and free concerts in its garden. Sometimes, the foundation also holds commemorative bashes, with free food, drinks, and live jams.

Keeping with the theme, you could make your next stop live venue **Buddy Guy's Legends**, the brainchild of its namesake Grammy-winning artist. The place is loaded with blues memorabilia and it welcomes impressive musical line-ups. Expect mostly local acts on weekdays and national performers on weekends.

Willie Dixon's Blues Heaven Foundation; 2120 S. Michigan Avenue; tel: 312-808-1286; www.bluesheaven. com; call for hours; charge; map G4 Buddy Guy's Legends; 700 S. Wabash Avenue; tel: 312-427-1190; www. buddyguys.com; Mon-Fri 11am-2am, Sat 5pm-3am, Sun 6pm-2am; charge; map F3

Hyde Park and the South Side

0   250   500 yds

0   250   500 m

N

Lake Michigan

Discover an **architectural masterpiece** at Frank Lloyd Wright's **Robie House**

Set on over 200 rambling acres in the Hyde Park neighborhood, the University of Chicago campus is loaded with structures of architectural interest, from its Collegiate Gothic Mitchell Tower – inspired by Oxford's Magdalen Tower – to its arts buildings fashioned by Ludwig Mies van der Rohe. Most notably, though, it's the site of Frank Lloyd Wright's **Robie House**. Listed on the National Register of Historic Places, it was designed in the architect's Oak Park studio, constructed between 1908 and 1910 and acquired by the university in 1963. Its design was informed by Wright's Ferdinand F. Tomek House in Riverside, Ill., and it was built for Frederick C. Robie, assistant manager of the Excelsior Supply Company in Chicago. Interestingly enough, though, he lived there with his wife, Laura, and two children for a mere 14 months. After a series of owners, it was sold to the Chicago Theological Seminary in 1926 and used as a dormitory and dining hall.

Over the years, to top it off, the building faced ruin more than once. Now safely in the hands of the Frank Lloyd Wright Preservation Trust, the Prairie-style masterpiece stands as one of America's architectural greats. In addition to offering interior tours – both guided and self-guided with audio – visitors can choose to take an in-depth tour of its private spaces. Workshops, twilight tours – complete with wine and beer – and after-hours gatherings with live music are options, too. Also, each Saturday at 1:30pm, interpreters host a mystery tour based on Blue Balliett's novel, *The Wright 3*. Whatever way you decide to experience the place, you'll be wowed by its details, from endless geometric art-glass windows to ambient lighting, created by the architect himself.

Fashioned as two side-by-side rectangles, it houses a billiards room, playroom, and enclosed garden, with living and dining rooms that flow one into the other, opening to a dramatic exterior balcony through a dozen glass-paneled French doors. Sweeping views can be seen from the third-floor bedrooms, and everything from a porch below a cantilevered roof to a coal storage room, second-story living and dining areas, and a workshop are located within.

Much of the building's original, Wright-designed

furniture is kept on campus at the **Smart Museum of Art** (5550 S. Greenwood Avenue; tel: 773-702-0200), including an oak armchair with metal feet, an oak dining room chair with a leather seat, and an armchair rocker. Sadly, little of it is actually on display. That said, the museum remains a worthy stop when on campus, given its collection of Asian, European, modern, and contemporary art.

Adding to its allure, gallery talks, concerts, and informative, art-filled afternoon get-togethers regularly take place. While meandering around, you'll also come across the **Oriental Institute** (1155 E. 58th Street; tel: 773-702-9514), a museum devoted to relics of the ancient Near East.

Courses, film screenings, lectures, and programming for all ages is available, though there's plenty to see just walking its galleries solo; there are ones dedicated to Egypt, Nubia, Persia, Mesopotamia, Syria, and Anatolia. See everything from funerary reliefs to Meroitic pottery and a Roman-era mummy of a five-year-old boy. Before leaving the campus, take time to eye Henry Moore's peculiar ***Nuclear Energy*** (north campus, 55th and 57th streets), a 1967 bronze sculpture erected to celebrate the splitting of the atom 25 years before.

Robie House; 5757 S. Woodlawn Avenue; tel: 312-994-4000; gowright. org/visit/robie-house.html; guided tours 11am–2pm Thur–Mon; charge; map D3

Take the kids to a game at **U.S. Cellular Field**, where access to a too-cool kid's club is free to ticket-holders

Located on the city's South Side, **U.S. Cellular Field** – formerly (and still often called) Comiskey Park – is the home of the Chicago White Sox. Opened in 1991 after the team spent 81 years at its old location, the Major League venue replaced what was then the oldest working ballpark in baseball. You can still see remnants of old Comiskey; the home plate is now a marble plaque on the sidewalk next to the park (north of the park, near Gate 5), and its foul lines have been painted in the parking lot. Beyond simply sitting in its stands, fans have oodles to keep them – or any young ones in tow – occupied.

Those 21-plus should consider making a stop at the **Bullpen Sports Bar**. Located next to the visitor's bullpen, it has a bi-level, open-air area with great views of the field (fees apply). Alternatively, family-friendly, 15,000-sq-ft (1,394-sq-m) **Fundamentals** in left field is a great kids' club manned by Chicago White Sox Training Academy coaches and free to ticket-holders. It gives kids the chance to field, pitch, run and hit speed pitches in batting cages free of charge – as long as they're wearing gym shoes.

The ballpark grub, meanwhile, is fabled. In addition to having top-tier hot dogs, there's multi-level, indoor-outdoor **Bacardi at the Park** (320 W. 35th Street; tel: 312-674-5860) from the Gibsons Steakhouse crew – accessible with or without a ticket. After the game, celebrate a win or swap stories with diehards at nearby **Schaller's Pump** (3714 S. Halsted Street; tel: 773-376-6332), a circa 1881 tap and former speakeasy with its original peephole intact.

U.S. Cellular Field; 333 W. 35th Street; tel: 312-674-1000; chicago.whitesox. mlb.com; dates and prices vary; map A2

Catch **off-the-radar** and lauded flicks at **DOC Films**

A gem of a find on the University of Chicago Campus in Hyde Park, **DOC Films** – or, more formally, the Documentary Film Group – is a film society run by students. Dating back to 1932, it began as a forum for documentaries, though genres now screened reach well beyond to include fictional and experimental movies. Screenings take place at Max Palevsky Cinema within Ida Noyes Hall. Over the years, directors from Alfred Hitchcock to John Ford and Woody Allen have come to lead discussions. It has also been the location of Chicago film premieres, such as *The Rules of the Game* and *Brokeback Mountain*. Delving deeper, its aficionado-friendly series focuses on artists, national cinemas, or genres, pulling from the country's top film archives.

Despite its serious street cred, DOC is also a place for casual flicksters to see straight-up screenings, attend special events and chat with directors, critics, and faculty members – all without breaking the bank. Beyond that, it's a spot to catch student creations via Fire Escape Films, a community of film-making students whose work has been featured at major film festivals. In addition to producing multiple shorts annually, it showcases some longer, narrative flicks made with professional-grade equipment.

Get ready for the show by grabbing a bag of popcorn at **Nuts on Clark** (Union Station, Adams and Canal streets) first. But beware: its famous caramel-and-cheese-corn is a many napkins affair. For something different to the norm, grab companion snacks, like sour gummy candy, from Hong Kong import **Aji Ichiban** (2117a S China Place; tel: 312-328-9998).

DOC Films; University of Chicago, Ida Noyes Hall, 1212 E. 59th Street; tel: 773-702-8575; docfilms.uchicago.edu; various days and times; charge; map D3

Keep winter chills at bay at **soul food** central, **Valois Cafeteria**

Despite some recent high-profile closures, Chicago's South Side is still the place to come for southern cooking, thanks to the district's black community that came north in the major social migration after World War II. Today, U of C students, professors and residents dig in to authentic soul food at cash-only Obama family fave **Valois Cafeteria.** The kind of place where time stands still, it's now a Chicago classic. The tagline 'See Your Food' hints at the experience: patrons line up – trays in hand – to procure temptations from a fully visible *smorgasbord* from morning until night. Start the day with French toast, a Denver omelet, and ham off-the-bone, contemplating a patty melt, roast pork sandwich, or hot beef with mashed potatoes and gravy as the day marches on.

The real draw, though, is the heart-warming – though certainly not diet-friendly – cafeteria-style specials, which include prime rib, baked pork chops, and beef goulash with noodles. Craving some mac and cheese? A hamburger 'steak' with onions? You'll find that, too, along with cream pies, cherry and peach cobbler, and hefty slices of cheesecake.

Depending on the time of day, you might also make your way to **Woodlawn Tap** (1172 E. 55th Street; tel: 773-643-5516; map D4), a legendary dive of a tavern frequented by a cross-section of patrons, including blue collar-types, students, and Nobel Peace prize winners, among them Saul Bellow. The bar – in the Chicago tradition – is long and narrow, with edibles limited to the likes of burgers. Don't get confused if you hear locals call it 'Jimmy's' after its late owner.

Valois Cafeteria; 518 E. 53rd Street; tel: 773-667-0647; www.valoisrestaurant. com; daily 5.30am–10pm; map A5

Explore the culturally rich **Bronzeville** neighborhood

To get orientated with the historic, culturally rich Bronzeville neighborhood, start at the **Bronzeville Information Center**. Residing within the Supreme Life Building at the gateway to the Black Metropolis Historic District, it offers a wealth of knowledge and a permanent gallery with temporary exhibits. Check out *Bronzeville to Harlem* by Preston Jackson, a bronze and steel interpretation of life here during the 1920s and 1930s. The center also offers tours with advance notice; topics range from the restoration of Bronzeville to a full-day exploration of Black Metropolis, the Great Migration, and the Blues Trail.

From there, stretch your legs at **Washington Park**, where Lorado Taft's 1920s-era *Fountain of Time* is located. The 102-foot-long (31m) sculpture overlooks a reflecting pool and features Father Time presiding over 100 figures. Listed on the National Register of Historic Places, the Frederick Law Olmsted-designed park also boasts an aquatic center with a 36-foot (11m) waterslide and an obstacle course at Bynum Island. It is also the site of the 1881 **Refectory** designed by Daniel H. Burnham, the **National Guard Armory**, and

several multi-cultural festivals and gatherings throughout the year.

Nearby, you'll find **Experimental Station**, where the 61st Street Farmers' Market and educational Blackstone Bicycle Works can be found. See, too, the **Urban Farm Project** at 61st Street and Dorchester Avenue, an organic community garden and quiet place to picnic and bask in the sun.

Bronzeville Visitor Information Center; 3501 S. Martin Luther King Drive, Suite 1 East; tel: 773 373-2842; Mon–Fri 11am–5pm; map A2
Washington Park; 5531 S. Martin Luther King Drive; tel: 773-256-1248; www. chicagoparkdistrict.com; map B3–B5
Experimental Station; 6100 S. Blackstone Avenue; tel: 773-241-6044; www.experimentalstation.org; map E2

Get some **peace and quiet** while celebrating the White City at **Jackson Park**

A 600-acre (243-hectare) sprawl on the South Side of Chicago, historic **Jackson Park** was the site of the World's Columbian Exposition of 1893. Laid out by Daniel Burnham and Frederick Law Olmsted, it featured 200 intentionally temporary, mostly neoclassical buildings, interspersed with lagoons and canals. The fair's impact on the city – and the world – was profound, spawning firsts from the Ferris wheel to Cracker Jack, picture postcards, and even spray painting. As told in *The Devil in the White City* by Erik Larson, the effort devoted to its success was unprecedented.

Originally built as the Palace of Fine Arts for the exposition, the Museum of Science and Industry is located in the only situated building that survived the fair. The structure later became the home of the Field Museum of Natural History, though the museum vacated the plaster-cast structure, and it was rebuilt in stone to house the **Museum of Science and Industry** (57th

Street and Lake Shore Drive; tel: 773-684-1414). Today, the **Field Museum of Natural History** is located down the street (1400 S. Lake Shore Drive; tel: 312-922-9410) and it dedicates a virtual museum to the fair.

Naturally, after the exposition closed, the grounds once again became landscaped parkland, with eastern and western climes connected by the grand Midway Plaisance. See its *Golden Lady* sculpture, a small-scale version of Daniel Chester French's *Statue of the Republic*; the original presided over the expo's Court of Honor. Other beloved antiquities include the calming, Japanese-style **Osaka Garden**, which was resurrected on its original site at Wooded Island after being vandalized during World War II. Reach the island from Hayes Drive, heading to the bridge on the north side of the lagoon, or commune with nature at the island's southern end. Among the animals to keep a lookout for while you're there are beavers, muskrats, and turtles, who live amid lush vegetation, like Jack-in-the-Pulpit, violets, and True and False Solomon's Seal.

Most of the island is considered part of the **Paul Douglas Nature Sanctuary**, a woodland, prairie, and shrub-filled bird habitat. Meanwhile, the Jackson Park lagoon is a popular place to fish for bluegill, and the park's **Bobolink Meadow** features a six-acre expanse filled with native species, birds, and butterflies. The park also features a harbor as well as two beaches: the **57th Street Beach**, known for its skyline views, and the **63rd Street Beach**, marked by a stunning Classical Revival-style pavilion. Beyond its walking, jogging, and running trails, the park has tennis courts, a playground, basketball courts, and baseball diamonds ~ not to mention a scenic spot to tee off. So pack a picnic and plan on an outdoorsy day.

Jackson Park; 6401 S. Stony Island Avenue; tel: 773-256-0903; www. chicagoparkdistrict.com; daily dawn–dusk; free; map F2

See **contemporary art** and attend lectures without spending a dime at the **Renaissance Society**

Using the University of Chicago campus as its base, the **Renaissance Society** is a free, open-to-the-public institution dedicated to contemporary art. Founded in 1915, it fosters an interest in rarely-seen works through vanguard visual arts exhibitions and events. In the 1920s and 1930s, the museum often procured works directly from the art studios of Picasso, Miró, and Mondrian. Its 1934 exhibition of Alexander Calder's mobiles and its 1936 showcase of Ferdnand Léger paintings were the first solo exhibitions of the artists in the United States.

From Ludwig Mies van der Rohe to Marc Chagall, Gertrude Stein, and Sergei Prokofieff, it has long been a spot to see forward-thinking works of art, though you can turn to it for concerts, movie screenings and lectures from contemporary artists, scholars and critics as well. Look, too, for insightful walk-throughs with artists when exhibitions first open, attend an avant-garde musical performance in Bond Chapel or Fulton recital hall, or take in an educational, professor-led talk.

Then, peer into the museum shop, where you'll find art books, gifts and exhibition posters. Continue on to unearth rare books and manuscripts at the campus-based **Special Collections Research Center** (1100 E. 57th Street; tel: 773-702-8705; map C4), which has an extensive archive on Chicago jazz. Or make your way to the soaring, six-story 'winter garden' at the **Charles M. Harper Center/Booth School of Business** (5807 S. Woodlawn Avenue; tel: 773-702-7743; map D3), grabbing a cup of coffee from the Everett Kovier Café while en route.

Renaissance Society; U of C, 5811 S. Ellis Avenue, Bergman Gallery, Cobb Hall 418; tel: 773-702-8670; www. renaissancesociety.org; Tue–Fri 10am–5pm, Sat–Sun noon–5pm; free; map C3

Explore **Kenwood** and **Pullman**, with a pick-me-up of clover coffee at **Zaleski & Horvath MarketCafe**

The quaint Kenwood district on the city's South Side is a pleasant place to ramble, and it's a delight of a destination for history enthusiasts. The home of many of Chicago's most successful businessmen and luminaries (architect Louis Sullivan, meatpacker Gustavus Swift) – not to mention America's 44th President, Barack Obama (5046 S. Greenwood Avenue), the residential neighborhood is also the site of **Rainbow PUSH Coalition** (930 E. 50th Street; tel: 773-373-3366), Rev. Jesse Jackson's headquarters. While it's not normally open to the public, the building does welcome visitors each Saturday at 10am for a live, public TV broadcast.

Before or after paying a visit, get a jolt at **Zaleski & Horvath MarketCafe**, an inviting deli with a large selection of global cheeses, sandwiches stuffed with artisanal goodies, and notable clover coffee. From there, head south to the **Historic Pullman District**, George Pullman's model town. Make your first stop the **Historic Pullman Foundation Visitor Center** (11141 S. Cottage Grove Avenue; tel: 773-785-8901; p.155), as it features an introductory video on the community's fascinating history, exhibits of Pullman-manufactured model trains, and various rail service memorabilia. It's also the starting point for monthly tours with experienced guides on first Sundays from May through October. They reveal not only the town's story but also the restoration efforts underway. However, it's also possible to grab a do-it-yourself walking tour brochure to go it alone.

Chicago Neighborhood Tours (tel: 312-742-1190; www.chicago neighborhoodtours.com) also offers insight into the Pullman district, departing from this address, with stops at Greenstone Church and the Hotel Florence.

Zaleski & Horvath MarketCafe; 1126 E. 47th Street; tel: 773-538-7372; www. zhmarketcafe.com; Mon–Fri 7am–7pm, Sat–Sun 8am–6pm; map B2

Admire the **skyline** from **Promontory Point**, then peruse the shelves in a good **bookstore**

When you need to get away from it all, head to naturalistic **Promontory Point**, the vision of landscape designer Alfred Caldwell. The Hyde Park haven – known locally as 'The Point' – is a man-made peninsula, built from landfill that juts out to Lake Michigan from Burnham Park. Dotted with serene gardens, it's fringed with fire pits along the lakefront and features running trails, beach access, and amazing views of the Chicago skyline. Surrounded by meadows, it also has a castle-like field house with stone verandas, which is used for special events.

Whether you opt to get active or sit and listen to the waves lap at the shore, there's something to suit every mood. Scout out the park's prairies and woodlands, filled with wildflowers – from black-eyed Susans to bee balm – as well as native birds and flitting butterflies,

LOCAL BOOKSTORES
If absorbing the view has put you in a mellow and introspective mood, head off to **57th Street Books** (1301 E. 57th Street; tel: 773-684-1300); buy, sell, or just browse at **Powell's Bookstore** (1501 E. 57th Street; tel: 773-955-7780), which is known for its philosophy, theology and collectible titles; or stop in **Seminary Co-op Book Store** (5757 S. University Avenue; tel: 773-752-4381) – it's intellect central for academia. For something travel-themed, make your way to **What the Traveler Saw** (1508 E. 55th Street; tel, 773-955-5055), a funky shop for international gifts, voyage-easing accessories and helpful info on packing, eating and sightseeing while on the road.

Then, walk the nature path at the north end of the parking lot, at 47th Street and Lake Shore Drive.

Promontory Point; 5491 S. South Shore Drive; tel: 312-747-6620; daily 7am–9pm; map F4

Learn about African-American culture at the
DuSable Museum of African American History

Named for Jean Baptiste Point DuSable, the Haitian of African and French heritage who established the trading post settlement that became Chicago, the **DuSable Museum of African American History** preserves and showcases the artifacts and chronicles the accomplishments of African Americans thorough time. Standing proud as the country's African-American museum of record, it has in its collection over 15,000 pieces, among them paintings, sculptures, and prints. It also offers family-friendly programming, including book signings, workshops, lectures, and cultural performances.

From a bust of its namesake to a replica trading post, profile-relief-style wooden murals depicting the arrival of Africans to North America, and portraits of prominent African-Americans in Illinois, the museum also features masks, textiles, and daily objects from the African continent. Beyond, find a gallery dedicated to African-Americans who served in the armed forces and an exhibition dedicated to the 42nd mayor of Chicago, Harold Washington. Wander further, and learn of the Civil Rights movement, and see works of art by Augusta Savage,

William H. Johnson, and Henry Tanner, along with pieces by Chicago artists Marion Perkins and Archibald Motley.

An appealing destination for children, the museum brings history alive through storytelling, illusions, and music-based performance as well as a museum-sponsored movie series held at Chicago's 120-plus parks. DuSable also holds a long-standing, annual arts and crafts festival the second weekend of July. It's dedicated to traditional, experimental, and ethnic works that underscore the museum's mission.

DuSable Museum of African American History; 740 E. 56th Place; tel: 773-947-0600; www.dusablemuseum.org; Tue–Sat 10am–5pm, Sun noon–5pm; charge; map B4

Stimulate your senses at the **Hyde Park Art Center**

Serving as the one of the oldest exhibition spaces in the city of Chicago, the **Hyde Park Art Center** has emphasized contemporary visual arts through exhibitions and educational programming since 1939. Whether it's an illusionary installation about vending machines or a show highlighting the distractions faced by modern youth culture, its shows are meant to provoke thought and spark discussion.

Be sure to visit its second floor space, site of a homespun, seasonal indoor and outdoor gardening exchange and rooftop garden – complete with seeds, houseplants, and Amish Friendship Bread starter. Take time to pick your own tomatoes,

paying what you procure by the honor system. Those who want to get their hands dirty can also sign up for one-day mini-courses and 'creative renewal' workshops that promote using new art mediums.

Alternatively, take a class on stained glass, bookbinding, or Afshar-style necklace making. During the summer, you can even send the kids to creativity camp, a hands-on experience with professional artists, loaded with outdoor play. Meanwhile, grown-ups can hit its open studio to paint and draw, provided you've signed up for a course. Additional resources include **4833**, a gathering place for students, artists and educators. When you're ready to head out, pay a visit to **The Fair Trader**, an eco-friendly, women-run retail store selling wares from Chicago artists, including jewelry and hand-batiked clothing.

Hyde Park Art Center; 5020 S. Cornell Avenue; tel: 773-324-5520; www. hydeparkart.org; various times and costs; map E5
The Fair Trader; 1623 E. 55th Street; tel: 773-966-5269; www. thefairtraderchicago.com; Mon–Fri 11am–6pm, Sat 10am–5pm; map E4

Play golf in the heart of the city, shaded by hardwoods, at the 18-hole Jackson Park Golf Course

Affordable with lovely Lake Michigan views, **Jackson Park Golf Course** is the perfect destination for golfing enthusiasts in search of an urban retreat. The city's pride and joy is this historic, 18-hole course, which is shaded by mature hardwood trees. There, a full bag of clubs is requisite since par 5s extend 560 yards and par 3s reach to 200 yards. Thankfully, it also houses a driving range for those who prefer to simply putt.

Annual tournaments are open to amateurs of all skill levels, though lessons – offered by the Chicagoland Golf Academy – are key for anyone hoping to improve their strokes. Offering beginner, intermediate, and advanced instruction at eight locations citywide, including at Jackson Park, it also schools kids and couples on the sport. While you can go with private instruction, group classes – both single-sex and mixed – are a great way to meet locals.

Other Chicago golf courses include **Robert A. Black Golf Course** (2045 W. Pratt Boulevard; tel: 312-742-7931), **Sydney R. Marovitz Golf Course** (3600 N. Recreation Drive; tel: 312-742-7930), **Columbus Park Golf Course** (5701 W. Jackson Boulevard; tel: 312-746-5573), and **Marquette Park Golf Course** (6700 S. Kedzie Avenue; tel 312-747-2761) as well as **Lincoln Park's Diversey Driving Range** (141 W. Diversey Parkway; tel: 312-742-7929), complete with 18-hole Diversey Miniature Golf. Additionally, there's a three-hole learning course, putting green and mini golf course at **Douglas Park** (1401 S. Sacramento Drive; tel: 312-747-7670), which is all-but-built for family fun.

Jackson Park Golf Course, 6401 S. Richards Drive; tel: 773-667-0524; www.cpdgolf.com; charge; map F1

Outlying Neighborhoods

Oak Park

Outlying Neighborhoods

E **F** **G** **H**

Kohl Children's Museum
Chicago Botanic Garden
Potbelly Sandwich Works
Yard House
Regal Glen Stadium 10 Theaters
Homer's Ice Cream
Baha'i House of Worship
Mary and Leigh Block Museum of Art

KENILWORTH
GILLSON PARK
GLENVIEW
Lake Ave
WILMETTE
GOLF
Central
EVANSTON
Dempster Street
Main
Street
Street
SKOKIE
Oakton
MORTON GROVE
NILES
DES PLAINES

Lake Michigan

5

4

W. Touhy Avenue
W. Devon Ave
West Peterson Avenue
JEFFERSON PARK
W. Foster Ave
RAVENSWOOD
ANDERSONVILLE
W. Lawrence Ave
UPTOWN
W. Montrose Ave
IRVING PARK
W. Irving Park Rd
LINCOLN PARK
W. Addison St
Wrigley Field
AVONDALE
LAKEVIEW
LOGAN SQUARE
W. Diversey Ave
LINCOLN PARK
W. Fullerton Ave
Lincoln Park Zoo
WICKER PARK
OLD TOWN
HUMBOLDT PARK
GOLD COAST
NEAR NORTH
Polish Museum of America
AUSTIN
LOOP
Garfield Park Conservatory
Willis Tower
GRANT PARK
Eisenhower Expressway
LITTLE ITALY
SOUTH LOOP
University of Illinois
PILSEN
CICERO
LAWNDALE
DOUGLAS PARK
BRIDGEPORT
Illinois Institute of Technology
Berwyn's Toy Trains & Models
Brookfield Zoo
RIVERSIDE
LYONS
STICKNEY
FOREST VIEW
Chicago Portage National Historic Site
Chicago Midway Airport
GAGE PARK
SUMMIT
CHICAGO LAWN
ENGLEWOOD
Pullman District
BEDFORD PARK
MARQUETTE PARK
ASHBURN

Chicago O'Hare International Airport
ROSEMONT
SCHILLER PARK
NORRIDGE
HARWOOD HEIGHTS
FRANKLIN PARK
ELMWOOD PARK
CRAGIN
STONE PARK
BELLWOOD
OAK PARK
see Oak Park Map
MAYWOOD
COLUMBUS PARK
FOREST PARK
BERWYN
WESTCHESTER
LAGRANGE PARK
WESTERN SPRINGS

Massa
Spizzico Pizzeria
Café Cubano
Johnnie's Beef
Amarind's

0   1   2 miles
0   1   2 km

3

2

1

155

Take comfort in **soul food** at **MacArthur's**, then visit some of Austin's **churches**

When nothing but a hefty helping of Southern comfort will do, make your way to **MacArthur's** in the Austin neighborhood. Serving in a simple, cafeteria-like setting, its granny stand-ins – baked or fried chicken, smothered pork chops, and meatloaf – are affordable, oversized, and doled out by a friendly, neighborhood staff. Specials change daily, so look forward to Fridays for barbecue turkey legs. But anytime is a good time to dine, since a roster of crowd-pleasers, like baked catfish, will always be on hand. Beyond these homespun dishes, there's little fuss – just a few salads; small or large sides like black-eyed peas, mac and cheese, and baked beans; and bread or muffins. And while it's pretty much impossible to save room for dessert, you should. The peach cobbler is the stuff of legends, and the banana pudding a fine specimen, too.

Because you'll need to walk off such a big meal, make a follow-up stop at ornate, English Gothic **St Martin de Porres Church**. The 12-story structure, designed by parish architect Karl M. Vitzthum, is where sun streams through a vibrant stained glass window of the Virgin Mary. Originally the St Thomas

Aquinas Church, it is ornamented with gargoyles, flying buttresses, and a Celtic cross.

From there, proceed to **Midway Park**, a three-block stretch in the Old Austin neighborhood. It's flanked with historic Victorian homes, has a large fountain and looms beneath iconic religious buildings – **Greater Holy Temple of God in Christ** and **St Martin's Episcopal Church** – which are located on either side.

MacArthur's; 5112 W. Madison Street; tel: 773-261-2316; daily 11am–9pm ; map C5
St Martin de Porres Church; 5112 W. Washington Boulevard; tel: 773-287-0206; smdp.archchicago.org; daily 9am–5.30pm; free; map C5
Midway Park; 5710 W. Midway Park; free; map B4

See **flourishing ferns** and arid desert plants at the **Oak Park Conservatory**

Oak Park is a thriving, artistic and open-minded community, easily accessed by the Blue and Green 'L' lines. Dotted with Frank Lloyd Wright residences, it's also the birthplace of author Ernest Hemingway. While the crowds flock to those spots, seek solace at the **Oak Park Conservatory**, a conservatory and botanic garden that dates back to 1914. Featuring 8,000 square feet of growing space, its experts coddle over 3,000 plants, some of them dating back to the building's original founding. Turn to its desert collection to see succulents, ereus opuntia, and pereskia.

Continuing on to its tropical room, the sound of exotic birds and trickling water gives way to a central koi pond filled with fish and turtles, shaded by a canopy of fig, banana, and papaya trees. Explore further and see *Monstera deliciosa*, a creeping vine that winds its way up Fiddle-Leaf figs. Meanwhile, watch for pilea, spider plants, and peperomia closer to the ground. From there, it's on to the fern room, where you'll find a bevy of impressive, ancient species, along with ponderosa lemon, sea grape, and rose apple trees.

Engage further with workshops and classes, covering topics like flower arranging and houseplant basics. Then, head down the road to play a board game – cup of Joe in hand – at community hangout, **Buzz Café**. Its organic menu emphasizes locally grown foods. It also serves a popular Sunday brunch, plying patrons with orange-battered French toast and apple-walnut-filled crepes. Watch, too, for a diverse line-up of events, including live music, spiritual readings, and knitting collectives.

Oak Park Conservatory; 615 Garfield Street, Oak Park; tel: 708-386-4700; www.oakparkparks.com; Mon 2pm-4pm, Tue-Sun 10am-4pm; free, suggested donation; map D3
Buzz Café; 905 S. Lombard Avenue, Oak Park; tel: 708-524-2899; thebuzzcafe.com; Mon-Fri 6am-9pm, Sat 7am-9pm, Sun 8am-2pm; map D3

Attend a **cooking class** – perhaps one that's bistro-themed for couples – at **Flavour Cooking School**

There's good reason to make the short trip to suburban Forest Park: friendly **Flavour Cooking School**, a technique-driven place teaching valuable kitchen know-how in a way that's straight-up fun. Depending on your speed and level of interest, sign up for a demonstration class, during which chefs prep grub and you watch, or opt for a hands-on course making posh patties, pasta, or stir frys of several kinds. Expertise-building classes – such as 'knife basics' or 'beef 101' – are geared toward beginners, while more confident learners may choose to can and preserve, cook lobster, or tackle Julia Child recipes, *Julie and Julia*-style.

The school also welcomes couples on bistro nights and kids during introductory classes

– they're for kitchen helpers as young as age four. Culinary kids' camps are ideal for families spending a bit of time around town, while family nights bring the generations together for tasty fun. Just traveling with the girls? Check out its 'porch shoes' series, when girls don their prettiest shoes and make porch-party-appropriate munchies. It's also worth watching for specials, since sometimes the cost of classes is dramatically reduced.

Flavour Cooking School; 7401 W. Madison Street; Forest Park; tel: 708-488-0808; www.flavourcookingschool. com; various times and prices; map C1

FOREST PARK RESTAURANTS

There's a bit of a restaurant and bar culture in Forest Park, so a visit here could conclude with a glass of wine and improvisational meal at **Gaetano's** (7636 W. Madison Street, Forest Park; tel: 708-366-4010; map C1); a serious pork chop with blue cheese potato salad at **SkrineChops** (7230 W. Madison Street, Forest Park; tel: 708-771-7230; map C1), where walls are marked by trophy animals; or drinks in the beer garden at **Duckfat Tavern & Grill** (7218 W. Madison Street, Forest Park; tel: 708-488-1493; map C2), a pub where pot roast nachos are an absolute must.

Take stock of Ernest Hemingway's literary legacy at the **Ernest Hemingway Museum and Birthplace Home**

American author, journalist, and Pulitzer and Nobel Prize winner Ernest Hemingway had a profound impact on 20th-century literature. Born and raised in suburban Oak Park in a Queen Anne-style house – now the **Ernest Hemingway Museum and Birthplace Home** – he went on to work as a reporter for the *Kansas City Star* and become an ambulance driver during World War I, a job that both injured him and inspired his novel, *A Farewell to Arms*.

Learn of his travels and works as you tour the parlor where his father gave music lessons and explore the tower where young Ernest kept wildlife specimens. Witness the formal library, masculine dining room, and the kitchen, used mostly by maids. Upstairs, a long hallway leads to six bedrooms, one the nursery where Ernest and his sister, Marcelline, slept in identical white cribs. From there, it's on to Mrs. Hemingway's room, where the first four of the family's six children were delivered by Dr Hemingway.

Next, take a short walk from his home to the museum, where permanent and temporary exhibits bring the author's legacy to life. You'll encounter both rare photos and his childhood diary as well as the famous letter from nurse Agnes von Kurowsky. Here's a spoiler for those not in the know: in it, she rejected him.

Ernest Hemingway Museum and Birthplace Home; 200 N. Oak Park Avenue, Oak Park; tel: 708-524-5383; www.ehfop.org; Sun–Fri 1–5pm, Sat 10am–5pm; charge; map B2

Quit counting calories and tuck in at the
Marion Street Cheese Market

A beloved destination for artisan charcuterie, cheese, and chocolate, **Marion Street Cheese Market** is an eco-minded, gourmet food store and restaurant with an approachable, yet upscale, feel. Peruse its top-shelf local and world-renowned cheeses, which are cut-to-order, along with craft beers and boutique wines, artisan pickles, and chocolates almost too pretty to eat (but inevitably devoured). Kitchen gadgets – coffee presses, cheese knives, or fondue pots – are available to buy from here too.

Upon sitting down in the restaurant, cheese-lovers will struggle to make a choice because of the delectable options available. It is advisable to start with pre-selected or customized cheese flights and snacks, like Gouda-crusted cashews and pretzel chips with dried apples, or Parmesan and cheddar cheese puffs. Several salads, from bison carpaccio to asparagus with egg and speck, are ideal for lighter appetites, while there are more substantial main courses as well, such as bacon-wrapped rabbit with caraway spaetzle. Note that festivities are frequently held in house, including wine and cheese pairings and live musical performances.

In the summer, stop by the store for posh picnics – maybe roasted tomato salad with pesto vinaigrette, a ham and cheese sandwich, and tart lemon bars – packed to enjoy at **Oak Park Festival Theatre's** outdoor Shakespearian performances, which are staged in nearby Austin Gardens (map B2).

Marion Street Cheese Market; 100 S. Marion Street, Oak Park; tel: 708-725-7200; www.marionstreetcheesemarket. com; cafe hours: lunch Mon–Fri 11am–3pm, dinner Sun–Wed 5–9pm, Thur–Sat 5–10pm, brunch Sat–Sun 9am–3pm; map C2

Explore what's in store at the **galleries** and **specialty boutiques** in the **Oak Park Arts District**

The arts are alive and well in the bustling community of Oak Park. Nowhere is this more evident than in the **Oak Park Arts District**, which spans several blocks and is filled with interesting galleries, specialty boutiques, and businesses, not to mention a variety of eateries. There are shops, including maternity fashions at **Majamas Boutique** (909 S. Lombard Avenue; tel: 708-524-9668); music or movement classes that can be taken whatever your age

at **Musikgarten of Oak Park** (344 Harrison Street; tel: 708-445-1633); and opportunities to make something artistic of your own. Try your hand at stained glass-making at **Morava Studios** (11 W. Harrison Street; tel: 708-383-9333).

Wandering the district, you can peer into working artists' studios, and see what's hung in galleries, like **Harrison Works** (17 Harrison Street; tel: 708-308-4602), which features the art of Elizabeth Gaylord and fellow creative-types. The third Friday of every month, a gallery walk takes place, and special activities – live music and classes – are held.

Finally, contemplate your art-centric day over some sake or a specialty martini at minimalist **Sen Sushi Bar** (814 S. Oak park Avenue; tel: 708-848-4400), specifically the 'ghost ship' maki, a mix of spicy tuna, sweet potatoes, cream cheese, scallions, and spicy mayo with a panko (breadcrumbs) crust. And be sure to follow it with an order of green tea *crème brûlée*.

Harrison Street, from Ridgeland Avenue to Austin Boulevard; www.oakparkartsdistrict.com; map D2–D4

Stop and smell the **flowers** at the **Chicago Botanic Garden**

Two-dozen fragrant gardens and four nature areas, set on 385 acres (156 hectares) – that's what a pitch-perfect day at the **Chicago Botanic Garden** entails. Never the same place twice, new flowers are constantly coming into bloom, and birds are ever flitting here, there, and everywhere before new ones take their place. Because the grounds are expansive, it's smart to hop aboard a 35-minute grand tram or bright encounters tour, the former offering a narrated overview, the latter taking a more detailed approach.

Whether your interest lies in dwarf conifers, gardens of the Great Basin, or bulbs, examples are bountiful, right alongside rose and sensory-themed gardens, as well as ones bursting with aquatic and semi-aquatic native plants, ornamental grasses, and irises. Seek inspiration from the heritage flowers, which pay homage to eras past; learn about aromatic herbs and juicy tomatoes, mingled with 400 kinds of edible plants; and access Evening Island, its stone pathways and terraces reached by one of two bridges.

But whatever you do, do not miss the **Japanese garden**, a symbolic, three-island stunner with hardscaping, pruned pines and Midwest-friendly plantings that reveal lake, grassland, and garden vistas. Not surprisingly, the picturesque botanic garden holds many events and offers a great deal of educational programming, from art festivals and photo walks to open-air chef demonstrations, a seasonal farmers' market, and live entertainment. Moreover, on the first and third Sundays from June through August, a free, one-hour musical performance takes place at 10am at the covered **McGinley Pavilion**; tunes emanate from the Esplanade on Tuesday evenings during summer; and Carillon bells ring for 45 minutes on Mondays from June through September at 7pm. Keep an eye out, too, for on-site farm dinners, when Chicago chefs prepare fare

from area farms and local beers, wines, and spirits are poured.

To say the least, the spot is kid-friendly as well, so get them involved in the regularly offered talks, story-times, and dances for wee ones. Lest you're left wondering, the gardens are a year-round destination; winter get-togethers may include birdhouse-making or snowflake explorations. Of course, options extend beyond what's before your eyes. Experts teach courses and are on hand to answer home gardening questions via a **plant hotline** (tel: 847-835-0972).

The gift shop is a fantastic resource as well, its shelves filled with not just nature-inspired trinkets but informational books about Illinois plants as well as invasive species. There's even a plant science library with upwards of 28,000 titles, 600 videos and DVDs, and 1,000 nursery catalogs. It also provides talks, whether specific to a genus or about the science of caring for rare book collections. Additionally, flower shows are hosted throughout the year. In other words, there's plenty of food for thought. Speaking of food, there's a **garden café** that divvies out fresh-made soups, salads, and sandwiches made largely from student-grown, local produce from Green Youth Farm.

Chicago Botanic Garden; 1000 Lake Cook Road, Glencoe; tel: 847-835-5440; www. chicago-botanic.org; daily 7am–9pm; charge; map F5 (off map)

Get the best Italian beef – and eat it **standing up** – at **Johnnie's Beef**

Before the doors even open, patrons line up for delicious Italian beef sandwiches at no-frills stand **Johnnie's Beef** in Elmwood Park, where the only physical seating involves a handful of tables outdoors. That is to say, you'll likely indulge in yours standing with others at the counter lining the compact, freestanding space. You'll have no trouble finding the joint, since its smoke scent can be detected from blocks away. This fact shines through in the hardwood-grilled Italian sausage sandwiches on offer, as well as the combos, which mix sizzling sausage and beef in a jus-dipped – and, preferably, giardiniera-topped – bun.

The other options here are numbered. However, while the pepper and egg sandwich and hot dog don't win best in show, they definitely hit the spot. The only fault to be found with the place, really, is its staffers' no-nonsense attitude. Nevertheless, don't leave without getting a generously packed cup of lemon ice for dessert, and remember to come with cash in hand. Since you may end up eating in your car, as many patrons do, think about grabbing a roll of paper towels

from the grocery store across the street; mess making is pretty much guaranteed.

If you seek more of a sit-down experience for your Italian foodie hit, several other nearby restaurants are worth visiting. On the short list is **Massa** (7434 W. North Avenue, Elmwood Park; tel: 708-583-1111; map F3), which is known for its paninis, great gelato, and pillowy, fried to order dough. Alternatively, turn to **Spizzico Pizzeria** (7446 W. North Avenue; tel: 708-583-0002; map F3), which specializes in pizza and wings.

Johnnie's Beef; 7500 W. North Avenue, Elmwood Park; tel: 708-452-6000; Mon–Sat 11am–midnight, Sun noon–midnight; map F3

Pay homage at the **Frank Lloyd Wright Home and Studio**, then attempt your own **creative works**

Serving as Wright's private residence and office for the first 20 years of his career, from 1889–1909, the **Frank Lloyd Wright Home and Studio** is where the fabled architect raised half-a-dozen children with his first wife. The home was constructed in a single year, when Wright was working for Louis Sullivan, his mentor. However, it remained a work in progress, with additions made to the property over the next eight years. It was here, in the studio, that Prairie style architecture was born and over 125 buildings, including the Robie House and Unity Temple, were designed. Take a guided tour through his sanctuary, taking note of the barrel-vaulted playroom and the octagonal balcony, which is suspended by chains. Be on the lookout for the village's annual Wright Plus architectural house-walk, which is usually held in May. It highlights homes in varying architectural styles around town.

Once you're sufficiently wowed, go on and take a jewelry class at **Bead in Hand**, a retail bead shop with every kind and color of bauble under the sun. Among the standouts is necklace-making for young beaders, bead knitting, bead crocheting, and ornament or napkin ring-making. Its experts will even let you use tools to repair jewelry on site, free of charge. Keep in mind that the store stays open until 8pm the third Friday of every month to participate in the regular gallery walk around the Oak Park Arts District (p.161).

Frank Lloyd Wright Home and Studio; 951 Chicago Avenue, Oak Park; tel: 708-848-1976; www.gowright.org; tours: daily 11am–4pm; charge; map B2
Bead in Hand; 145 Harrison Street, Oak Park; tel: 708-848-1761; www.beadinhand.com; Mon–Tue 10am–6pm, Thur 10am–7pm, Fri 10am–6pm, Sat 10am–5pm, Sun noon–5pm; various times and prices; map D3

Act like a kid at – or bring yours along to – the **Kohl Children's Museum**

Housed in a modern, entertainment-packed indoor-outdoor space in Glenview, the **Kohl Children's Museum** is engaging for all ages. Get wet at Water Works, where sprayers propel pinwheels and boats bobble down canals; check out books like a librarian; and make play sandwiches at a mock-up of local sub shop Potbelly Sandwich Works. From there, try your hand at being a vet, or shop the aisles – and stand in as cashier – at a model Dominick's grocery store. Kids will appreciate 'stopping by' the Willis Tower Geoscraper or pretending they're at the John Hancock Center, where cranking a wheel generates electricity. There's plenty of teamwork involved, too: peddle bikes at Cooperation Station spring balls like popcorn from all angles.

At the same time, music-makers can busy themselves by making masterpieces at the section for things percussion and string, while learning about melody, harmony and rhythm. Outside, when the weather cooperates, you'll find cool, climbable structures, a sculpture trail and an underground tunnel that begs for peek-a-boo.

Although there's a café on site, a better bet is to continue down Patriot Boulevard for a meal. The Glen Town Center is full of options, including an actual **Potbelly Sandwich Works** (1840 Tower Drive, Glenview; tel: 847-729-3719; map F5), which proves a perfect precursor to movies at the **Regal Glen Stadium 10 Theatres** (1850 Tower Drive Glenview; tel: 847-729-9600).

Kohl Children's Museum; 2100 Patriot Boulevard, Glenview; tel: 847-832-6600 www.kohlchildrensmuseum.org; Mon 9.30am–noon, Tue–Sat 9.30am–5pm, Sun noon–5pm, with expanded hours during summer; charge; map F5

Get **homemade scoops** at a vintage parlor, then explore the **Wilmette** neighborhood

Just a short ride from the Kohl Children's Museum is Wilmette's historic **Homer's Ice Cream**. Its home-made scoops may make it on to many Chicagoland dessert menus, but they taste best of all when they're procured directly from the source. Standing in its original location since opening in 1935, it's rumored Al Capone – whose lake home was nearby – frequently came to indulge. Its name has a bit of curiosity, too. It honors the donkey that the original owner Gus Poulos sold, in order to pay for his trip here from Greece.

Step up to the counter of the vaguely carnival-esque scooper, choosing between rum raisin, ultra-fresh peach or Burgundy cherry, made with dark Bordeaux cherries from France. If you're looking to go fancy, creamy caramel or pineapple sundaes are tough to beat, though choices run the gamut and include rainbow sherbet, Champagne sorbet, and an edited selection of frozen yogurt. Admittedly, though, ordering anything but the main attraction would be something of a shame.

If you're making a day of things, consider other addresses of interest in the Wilmette area,

Baha'i House of Worship

such as the **Baha'i House of Worship** (100 Linden Avenue, Wilmette; tel: 847-853-2300; map H5), one of only seven such temples built in the world, as well as the oldest. The Baha'i faith emphasizes the 'oneness of God' and the structure's lacey designs incorporate symbols of the world's major religions. Alternatively, visit **Gillson Park** (Sheridan Road and Michigan Avenue, Wilmette; tel: 847-256-9656; map H5), which affords beachfront activities, such as swimming and sailing, as well as active fun at a lighted ice rink and tennis courts.

Homer's Ice Cream; 1237 Green Bay Road, Wilmette; tel: 847-251-0477; www.homersicecream.com; Sun–Thur 11am–10pm, Fri–Sat 11am–11pm, one hour later in summer; map G5

Play with **model trains and quirky toys** whether you're young or old

Casual and serious collectors converge at **Berwyn's Toy Trains & Models**, its shelves towering with tank engines. Since young ones can't exactly sit on their hands, interactive train tables with plenty of bridges, buttons, twists, turns and tunnels provide a release. In the back, a working electric train runs through a miniature village; again, there are buttons for hands-on fun. Although wheeled wonders are certainly its focus, a huge selection of Playmobil and Erector sets, Ty stuffed animals, and Breyer horses prove this is no one-trick pony.

While it's hard to tear oneself – or one's kids – away, there's more entertainment to be found at retro toy and oddity store **Pumpkin Moon** (1028 North Boulevard, Oak Park; tel: 708-524-8144; map B2), located in Oak Park. Ware include eye robots that make sparks, strange baby dolls and gag gifts, like bacon-flavored lip balm and rubber chickens. There are oodles of wind-ups, too, as well as kazoos, Bozo bop bags, and bump 'n go spaceships. At the same time, you'll be tempted to buy friction-powered rockets and tin cars, or for something kookier, weird whistles, a Hillary Clinton nutcracker, and funny t-shirts fit the bill.

Should you get bored – though it's hard to imagine you will – walk to the **Book Table** (1045 Lake Street, Oak Park; tel: 708-386-9800; map B2) for a quaint print-buying experience or see what's on the racks at women's boutique, **Muse** (106 N. Marion Street, Oak Park; tel: 708-948-7052; map B2).

Berwyn's Toy Trains & Models; 7025 Ogden Avenue, Berwyn; tel: 708-484-4384; www.berwynstoytrains.com; Mon and Thur 10am-7.30pm, Tue-Wed and Fri 10am-6pm, Sat 10am-5pm; map F2

Get to know **sculpture** at the **Mary and Leigh Block Museum of Art**

Located on the Northwestern University campus, the **Mary and Leigh Block Museum of Art** focuses on the visual arts, hanging several exhibitions annually and organizing numerous lectures, while hosting symposia and artist and scholar-manned workshops. Check out the prints and photographs, a collection that includes Jasper Johns' 1971 *Decoy*, a color lithograph and die cut. Well-represented are European prints and drawings from Old Masters to the 19th century, including numbers from Rembrandt, William Hogarth, and Albrecht Dürer. They offer a nice counterpoint to more contemporary 20th and 21st-century imagery, including Max Beckmann's *On the Streetcar*, a 1922 drypoint. You'll also come across plenty of work from independent photographers and photojournalists as well as architectural drawings from Walter Burley Griffin. But don't ignore the lesser-known Chicago artists, whose work is represented from 1935 to the present.

That said, no trip is complete without a walk through the museum's sprawling sculpture garden. Barbara Hepworth's cast bronze *Two Forms (Divided Circle)* can be viewed along with creations from Joan Miró and Henry Moore. The museum also screens classic and contemporary films at its **Block Cinema**, some of them rare films from the Baseball Hall of Fame. During the summer, the cinema also features free, thematic outdoor movies, showing them along the lakefront.

Mary and Leigh Block Museum of Art; 40 Arts Circle Drive, Evanston; tel: 847-491-4000; www.blockmuseum. northwestern.edu; Tue–Sun 10am–5pm; free tours; map H5

169

hotels

The city of Chicago has all manner of accommodations – from ones that are sky-high in every sense to locales for budget-minded stays. Hotel room rates include taxes and occasionally complimentary Wi-fi, but guests can count on paying more for parking and conveniences like bottled water. However, better deals can usually be negotiated with advance purchase online.

Many properties are concentrated in the bustling central business district of the Loop and on the main shopping drag, the Magnificent Mile, including landmark structures with stories to tell. However, you'll also find boutique hotels tucked onto stylish, tree-shaded residential streets in and around Oak Street.

Scene-seekers will find plenty to love at fashion-forward hubs, marked by lounge-like lobbies, rooftop bars, and restaurants from notable chefs; most of these are found in the heart of downtown. Even eco-conscious travelers can take comfort knowing there are intimate hotels, carved from sustainable materials, in close proximity to city attractions. Depending on your vision of the perfect view, snag a park-facing room along Michigan Avenue, or to see soaring skylines, take to the Gold Coast area, splurging on gracious, sweeping accommodations with loads of panache.

Admittedly, the less central communities have few places to stay, save a pleasant option in Lincoln Park, but public transportation makes it easy to get from point A to point B.

HOTEL PRICES

Price for an average room in high season, including 15.4% Chicago hotel tax but not including breakfast

$$$$ over $350
$$$ $180–350
$$ $100–180
$ under $100

Landmark Hotels

Palmer House Hilton
The Loop
17 E. Monroe Street; tel: 312-726-7500;
www.hilton.com; map p.87 F4; $$
Traditional grandeur is marked by
a soaring lobby and a Beaux Arts
ceiling, restored by a Sistine Chapel
artist. Guests of this historic hub will
find modern, renovated rooms – some
with two bathrooms – furthered by a
posh, 11-room penthouse suite with
more comforts than the average home.
Beyond its pool, on-site shopping, and
fitness center, there's Lockwood, a
Modern American restaurant of note.

The Drake
Magnificent Mile
140 E. Walton Place; tel: 312-787-2200;
www.thedrakehotel.com; map p.61 F5; $$
This Italian Renaissance-style, 1920s
hotel keeps comfort at the forefront,
from its clubby Palm Court lobby,
where high tea is held, to its seafood-
centric Cape Cod Room, and elegant
rooms with plush beds and fancy
furnishings. Not surprisingly, it's long
been a favorite with luminaries, such
as Winston Churchill, Frank Sinatra,
and Marilyn Monroe.

Hotel Burnham
The Loop
1 W. Washington Street; tel: 312-782-1111;
www.burnhamhotel.com; map p.87 E4; $$
Boutique-y with a history to tell,
this property is set within the
1895 Reliance Building. Restored
and turned into a hotel in 1999, it
maintains many of its original details,
from the colorful mosaic ceiling and
walls to the ornate metal elevator
grills. Its inviting rooms, nestled in
the heart of the hubbub, exude luxury
with rich gold and blue hues, pillow
menus, and mahogany furniture.

Millennium Knickerbocker Hotel Chicago
Magnificent Mile
163 E. Walton Place; tel: 312-751-8100; www.
millenniumhotels.com; map p.61 G5; $$
Steps from Water Tower Place and
Michigan Avenue shopping, this
elegant, 14-story, Gothic-inspired pad
opened its doors as the David Hotel in
1927. According to rumor, Al Capone's
brother ran a casino and speakeasy on
its penthouse floor during Prohibition.
Nowadays, its luxury rooms and suites
have all you could want, including
cushy robes and slippers, premium
pillow-top beds, and 40-inch LCD TVs.

Money No Object

Four Seasons Chicago
🟦 Magnificent Mile

120 E. Delaware Place; tel: 312-280-8800;
www.fourseasons.com/chicagofs; map p.61
F4; $$$$

Some come to this refined locale for
its serene spa and restaurant alone. Its
guest rooms, though, are nothing to
sniff at, with their sweeping lake or city
views and mid-20th-century French
décor, marble-swathed bathrooms,
LCD TVs, and Wi-fi access. The hotel
also has a pool and fitness facilities.

Trump International Hotel & Tower Chicago
🟦 River North

401 N. Wabash Avenue; tel: 312-588-8000;
www.trumpchicagohotel.com; map p.60
B1; $$$$

This 1,170ft (357m) behemoth
dominates the Chicago skyline,
offering great views. The second-tallest
building in the US, it has a spa, 339
luxury rooms, and the lauded Sixteen
restaurant. Rooms are sunlight-
drenched with floor-to-ceiling windows
and suites boast full kitchens.

The Elysian
🟦 Gold Coast

11 E. Walton Street; tel: 312-646-1300;
www.elysianhotels.com; map p.61 E5; $$$$

This haute 188-room hotel and
residence sports distinctive private
spaces with Carrera marble bathrooms
including soaking tubs and separate
showers, beds enveloped in 460-thread-
count Italian linens, fireplaces, and
furnished terraces. Accordingly, there is
a top-tier spa and health club, plus two
touted restaurants: Balsan and Ria.

Ritz-Carlton Chicago
🟦 Magnificent Mile

160 E. Pearson Street; tel: 312-266-1000;
www.fourseasons.com/chicagorc; map p.61
G4; $$$$

This hotel's name is synonymous
with luxury, a fact that its setting atop
Water Tower Place amply delivers on.
In addition to having a pool, sauna,
whirlpool, and gym, it gives guests
complimentary internet access in
its rooms, all of which are framed
by large picture windows and have
premium down pillows and duvets.

Boutique Hotels

The James
🔲 River North

55 E. Ontario Street; tel: 312-337-1000; www.jameshotels.com/Chicago; map p.60 C2; $$$

Situated steps from the Mag Mile, Millennium Park, and the Museum of Contemporary Art, this modern hotel has it all: rooms with plasma TVs, MP3 docks, slate-tile and marble bathrooms, and eco-friendly bedding in standard, studio-loft, one bedroom suite, and penthouse configurations.

Hotel 71
🔲 The Loop

71 E. Wacker Drive; tel: 312-346-7100; www.hotel71.com; map p.87 F5; $$

Having undergone a major renovation, this intimate, 39-story property is within walking distance of shopping, the business district, and some of Chicago's top dining establishments. A residential feel pervades, with hardwood details and marble foyers. Its deluxe and premier rooms are more spacious and afford the best views, along with perks like iPod docking stations. Be sure to hit the happy hour at in-house Hoyt's for fab deals.

Dana Hotel and Spa
🔲 River North

660 N. State Street; tel: 312-202-6000; www.danahotelandspa.com; map p.60 B2; $$$

Capped by the stylish Vertigo Sky Lounge, this ultra-hip haunt is swathed with sustainable woods, hand-hewn floors, and floor-to-ceiling windows. Rooms come outfitted with spacious rain-showers, Bowers & Wilkins sound systems, and chilled-in-room vinos waiting to be poured. Upgraded rooms even have two-person showers with 'floating' stone benches.

theWit
🔲 The Loop

201 N. State Street; tel: 312-467-0200; www.thewithotel.com; map p.86 E5; $$$

In the heart of the theater district with panoramic city views, this 27-story hotel with a bold yellow facade is a hotspot with notable restaurants and a destination lounge, ROOF. Pleasures include the multimedia theater, intimate urban spa, and glam rooms with luxury bedding, high-def entertainment centers, and spa-inspired bathrooms, including Gilchrist & Soames amenities.

Heart of the Action

Fairmont Chicago
The Loop
200 N. Columbus Drive; tel: 312-565-8000;
www.fairmont.com/chicago; map p.87 G5;
$$$
Walk to Grant and Millennium Parks
from this business-friendly hotel,
where oversized rooms are hung with
original floral art and feature marble
bathrooms with separate walk-in
showers and gracious views of the
parks or lake. Discerning travelers,
too, will appreciate its 700-sq-ft (65-sq-
m) suites with wet bars and fireplaces.
Set within its dramatic lobby is
ENO's wine bar (p.75), which serves
flights of wine, chocolate, and cheese.
Alternatively, aria restaurant tempts
with modern Asian eats.

Sofitel Chicago Water Tower
Gold Coast
20 E. Chestnut Street; tel: 312-324-4000;
www.sofitel.com; map p.61 E4; $$$
Located amid Rush Street nightlife
and Oak Street shopping, this 32-floor,
prismatic, architectural gem has urban-
chic rooms featuring Bose systems
and marble bathrooms with glass
showers and bathtubs. Some overlook
the city, while others offer partial Lake
Michigan views. When staying here,
roll out of bed for croissants at on-site,
French-leaning Café des Architectes.

Conrad Chicago
Gold Coast
521 N. Rush Street; tel: 312-645-1500; www.
conradchicago.com; map p.60 C1; $$$
A residential vibe greets guests of
this modern, conveniently poised
hotel in what was once the McGraw-
Hill Building. Marked by exterior
sculptures by Gwen Lux, its comfy-
cool rooms and suites sport 42-inch
plasmas, iPod alarm clocks, and Bose
entertainment systems as well as
deep soaking tubs. Grab a cocktail –
or watch a Sunday night movie with
surround sound – on its terrace lounge.

Rooms With a View

Renaissance Blackstone Hotel
■ The Loop
636 S. Michigan Avenue; tel: 312-447-0955;
www.blackstonerenaissance.com; map p.87
F2; $$$

Located downtown overlooking Grant
Park, this hotel is hung with over
1,400 works by Chicago artists, while
rooms have pillow-top mattresses,
stereo systems, marble bathrooms
with bathrobes, and iPod docking
stations. An on-site fitness center
features cardio equipment and free
weights, while kaleidoscopic Mercat
a la Planxa restaurant offers cool
indulgence with shareable Catalan
plates – including an advance-order
pig roast that could feed a small army.

InterContinental Chicago
■ Magnificent Mile
505 N. Michigan Avenue; tel: 312-944-4100;
www.icchicagohotel.com; map p.60 C1; $$$

Step in right off Michigan Avenue
and be enveloped in the comfort of
this dual-tower property. Clock details
such as carved reliefs in Assyrian-
style limestone and revel in the
contemporary-meets-classic rooms,
which embrace 1920s style, with
adornments ranging from murals to
regal draperies, plus modern amenities
and impressive views of the city or lake.

W-Hotel Chicago Lakeshore
■ Streeterville
644 N. Lake Shore Drive; tel: 312-943-9200;
www.starwoodhotels.com/whotels/index.
html; map p.61 E2; $$$

The city's Lake Michigan-facing
hotel is also one of its most scenester-
populated. Notable for its signature
Bliss spa, it also has a chill, DJ-manned
living room for cocktails, a rooftop
lounge with twinkling views, and the
global-Mediterranean Wave restaurant.
In rooms and suites, find signature
bedding, comfy chaise longues, LCD
flat-screens, and Bliss bath amenities.

Family-Friendly

The Peninsula Chicago
🟦 River North

108 E. Superior Street; tel: 312-337-2888; www.peninsula.com/Chicago; map p.60 C2; $$$$

Book a family fun package at this swanky Far East-inspired spot, or zero in on available perks, such as PlayStations, coloring books, and board games. Kids can also take baking classes or go on scavenger hunts, and parents can bask in the luxury of extra-spacious rooms and suites with marble bathrooms and soaking tubs with personal TVs. Multiple dining venues ensures there's something for all.

Park Hyatt Chicago
🟦 Magnificent Mile

800 N. Michigan Avenue; tel: 312-335-1234; www.parkchicago.hyatt.com; map p.60 C3/ p.61 F4; $$$

Pamper yourself by taking less luggage; baby and toddler necessities can be waiting in your room with advance notice. There's plenty for grown-ups to enjoy too, including hypoallergenic rooms with DVD players, not to mention picturesque NoMI Garden, a remote-feeling, seventh-floor retreat.

Hotel Monaco
🟦 The Loop

225 N. Wabash Avenue; tel: 312-960-8500; www.monaco-chicago.com; map p.87 F5; $$

Amenities for babies, tots, and kids range from high-chairs to lists of kid-friendly destinations and child-size robes, easing the burden of packing for traveling families. Solo travelers and couples are welcomed too, with in-room spa services, colorful accommodations with Frette linens, and 24-hour room service from South Water Kitchen.

Affinia Chicago
🟦 Magnificent Mile

166 E. Superior Street; tel: 312-787-6000; www.affinia.com/Chicago; map p.60 C2; $$

Tucked just off frenetic Michigan Avenue, this stylish retreat's rooms have complimentary experience kits (choose the BYOB version or the one with a loaned, pre-loaded iPod shuffle and guidebook of walking tours). In-room spa treatments are perfect for indulging, while access to a board game-filled family fun chest and stocked, kid-friendly backpack means everyone feels looked after.

Affordable Style

Hotel Felix
River North
111 W. Huron Street; tel: 312-447-3440; www.hotelfelixchicago.com; map p.60 A2; $$
Eco-friendly, luxurious and budget-friendly at once, this happening hotel is set within the gallery district and is close to the city's most legendary theaters and boutiques. City-view rooms continue the theme with luxury bedding, iPod docks, and designer toiletries – as well as room service from organic-minded Elate and services from an on-site spa.

The Whitehall Hotel
Gold Coast
105 E. Delaware Place; tel: 312-944-6300; www.thewhitehallhotel.com; map p.61 F4; $$
European charm benchmarks this small, centrally located property decked with glinty chandeliers, wood paneling, and tufted leather chairs. Guest rooms and suites offer cashmere Hypnos mattresses, terry cloth bathrobes, and mosaic-tiled marble bathrooms.

The Allerton Magnificent Mile
Magnificent Mile
701 N. Michigan Avenue; tel: 312-440-1500; www.theallertonhotel.com; map p.60 C2; $
This sleek, budget-friendly spot is a 1920s Italian Renaissance-style keepsake with fully modern appointments, including rooms and suites with MP3 docking stations, marble bathrooms, and 325-thread-count sheets on cushy beds.

Hilton Garden Inn Chicago Magnificent Mile
Magnificent Mile
10 E. Grand Avenue; tel: 312-595-0000; www.hiltongardeninn.com; map p.60 B1; $$
You don't have to spend a lot to benefit from a central locale. That's evidenced by this downtown hotel with an indoor pool, hot tub, and wildly popular Weber Grill restaurant. The guest rooms don't disappoint either, with creature comforts like compact refrigerators and microwaves as well as Willis Tower or John Hancock Center views.

Tremont Hotel
Gold Coast
100 E. Chestnut Street; tel: 312-751-1900; www.starwoodhotels.com; map p.61 F4; $$
This elegant, intimate hotel's rooms feature sitting areas, flat-screen TVs, and marble bathrooms. Meanwhile penthouse suites boast fireplaces and wet bars. All feature complimentary Wi-fi access. For some local sports history, stop by Mike Ditka's, Iron Mike's bi-level steakhouse that's adorned with prized sports collectibles.

Urban Hideaways

The Belden-Stratford Hotel
Lincoln Park
2300 Lincoln Park West; tel: 773-281-2900;
www.beldenstratfordhotel.com; map p.45
E4; $$

These luxury apartments and suites
– complete with crown molding,
spacious kitchens, and elevated
ceilings – are set within a historic
building overlooking the Lincoln
Park Conservatory. Appealing perks
range from an on-site laundry and
dry cleaning to a fitness center,
full-service salon, and furnished
rooftop deck overlooking the park.
Plus, its dining is noteworthy. On
the casual end, Mon Ami Gabi
affords great takes of French bistro
faves, while storied seafooder L2O
wows consistently with its intricate
onslaught of creative plates.

The Essex Inn
The Loop
800 S. Michigan Avenue; tel: 312-939-2800;
www.essexinn.com; map p.87 F2; $$

There's plenty of culture surrounding
this cost-conscious property
graced with vistas of Grant Park,
the Museum Campus, and Lake
Michigan. Guests enjoy free Wi-fi
throughout the hotel, while reveling
in rooms hung with Art Institute
reproductions and outfitted with LCD
flat-screens, iPod docks, and ample
workspaces. Other highlights include
a sunny, all-season rooftop pool
and outdoor garden, plus a fitness
center, 24-hour business center, and
complimentary shuttle service to the
Magnificent Mile, Museum Campus,
and Navy Pier. Don't forget to check
out its buzzy, sustainably minded
restaurant, Tribute.

Essentials

A

Age Restrictions
The legal drinking age is 21, and it is strictly enforced. Many bar and restaurant proprietors will check people who appear 35 years and younger. Always carry identification.

Airports and Arrival
Chicago is serviced by two major airports. **O'Hare International**, 17 miles (27km) northwest of downtown, is a major flight hub and one of the busiest airports in the world. The cheapest and often most efficient method of getting to and from O'Hare is the 'L;' the Blue line runs 24 hours a day, with trains every eight to 10 minutes. The trip downtown takes about 50 minutes, with departure from a station near the elevators to the main parking garage. You can opt to buy a CTA Transit Card or unlimited ride pass using cash (machines do not give change) or credit/debit cards at both airport train stations. A taxi ride to downtown costs around $35-$40.

Midway International Airport, 12 miles (19km) southwest of downtown, is smaller and serves mainly budget airlines. It is accessible via the 'L's Orange line, taking about 45 minutes.

Airport Express (tel: 888-284-3826; www.airportexpress.com) provides shuttle service between both airports and major downtown hotels; the cost of a one-way ticket for a single customer is $29 to O'Hare, $24 to Midway.

Amtrak trains depart and arrive at downtown's **Union Station** (225 S. Canal Street; tel: 312-655-2066 or 800-872-7245; www.amtrak.com) and serve regional and national destinations. The Clinton stop on the Blue line is the closest 'L' station.

Greyhound buses are a cheaper but less comfortable option than train or air. The main station is at 630 W. Harrison St. (tel: 312- 408-5821; www.greyhound.com), and the closest 'L' stop is the Blue Line's Clinton station.

B

Business Hours
Businesses and government offices in Chicago are generally open from 9am to 5pm Monday to Friday. Banking hours are generally 8.30am to 5pm, with many branches open on Saturdays and several open on Sundays.

C

Car Rentals
Driving in the downtown area is not necessary or advised. Should you wish to explore farther afield, however, car rental agencies are located throughout the city and at the airports. Drivers must be at least 21 and have a driver's license and a valid credit card.

Climate and Clothing
Spring is often rainy and gray but is relieved by perfect 75°F (24°C) days. Summer can be stiflingly hot and

humid with temperatures exceeding 90°F (32°C); night-time temperatures seldom drop below 70°F (21°C). Autumn is pleasant, with crisp sunny days, moderate temperatures, and colorful fall foliage. Winter, especially January and February, is brutally cold, with below-freezing temperatures, biting winds, and desolate streets. For updated information, visit www.weatherpages.com/chicago.

Chicago weather is extreme and unpredictable, with four clearly defined seasons. Dressing in layers is highly recommended. Frequent and extreme temperature changes, often within just a few hours, can leave you shivering or sweltering unexpectedly. Dress codes in Chicago vary, though it is not uncommon to see business casual attire worn in upscale restaurants. There are exceptions: sophisticated establishments may require a jacket and tie for men and equally smart attire for women.

Consulates
Australia: 123 N. Wacker Drive, Suite 1330, tel: 312-419-1480.
Canada: Two Prudential Plaza, 180 N. Stetson Avenue, Suite 2400, tel: 312-616-1860.
Ireland: 400 N. Michigan Avenue, Suite 911, tel: 312-337-1868.
New Zealand: 8600 W. Bryn Mawr Avenue, Suite 500N, tel: 773-714-9461.
UK: Wrigley Building, 13th floor, 400 N. Michigan Avenue, Suite 1300, tel: 312-970-3800.

Crime and Safety
Like fellow modern cities, Chicago experiences its share of crime. Consequently, common sense should prevail at all times. In close proximity, it is typical to find wealthy enclaves that give way to more questionable blocks. Chicago crime has fallen over recent years, but it's best to exercise caution when venturing out – especially after dark.

Customs
Information on regulations and restrictions when entering the US is available at www.customs.ustreas.gov. Only people 21 years old and over may bring alcohol and tobacco into the US. Meat and dairy products, seeds, plants, fruits, and Cuban cigars are not permitted into the US.

D

Disabled Access
See www.accessiblechicago.org, which provides a rating system of disabled-friendly facilities and activities in the city. General information and tips on mobility-impaired travel throughout Illinois can be found at www.vacationsmadeeasy.com/chicago and www.globalaccessnews.com. A list of hotels in Chicago detailing accessible facilities can be found at www.access-able.com.

There are many Chicago tour organizations that specifically cater to disabled travelers. For neighborhood tours, **Walk Chicago Tours** (www.

walkchicagotours.com) will custom design itineraries for disabled visitors. For boat trips, **Lucky Dog Charters** (www.luckydogcharters.com) can accommodate three wheelchair users per excursion.

The CTA has information on stations and services that are wheelchair accessible: www.transit chicago.com/maps/accessible.html.

Discounts
City Pass, tel: 888-330-5008, www. citypass.com. Valid for nine days, City Pass permits entry to six attractions. It can be purchased online, by phone, or at any of the participating attractions.
Chicago Plays, tel: 312-554-9800, www. chicagoplays.com. The League of Chicago Theatres, which has almost 200 members ranging from small companies to the major 'Broadway in Chicago' venues, offers the Hot Tix discount ticket program.
Go Chicago Card, tel: 866-628-9031, www.gochicagocard.com. This flexibility card is available in one-, two-, three-, five-, or seven-day increments and includes more than 25 attractions. Purchasing and presenting a Go Chicago Card entitles the holder to discounts of up to 20 percent.

E
Electricity
Standard American electric current is 110 volts with two-pin plugs. Adapters will be required for foreign visitors. Standard European is 220-240 volts.

Emergencies
For police, ambulance or fire, dial 911. Do not leave the scene of an auto accident until the police arrive.

Entry and Regulations
For a breakdown of up-to-date US entry regulations, visit http://travel. state.gov. For visa inquiries, tel: 202-663-1225; email: usvisa@state.gov.

H
Health and Medical Care
There is a limited public health care system in the US. Should you require medical assistance, you will need to present your insurance information or pay for treatment at the time of your visit. Always attempt to contact your insurance company before you receive treatment; many companies require immediate notification and may require that you receive treatment at designated hospitals. For immediate attention, dial 911 or go directly to a hospital emergency room. There are 24-hour emergency centers at the hospitals citywide, including:
John H. Stroger Jr. Hospital: 1900 W. Polk Street, tel: 312-864-6000, www. johnstrogerhospital.org
Northwestern Memorial Hospital: 251 E. Huron Street, tel: 312-926-2000, www.nmh.org
Rush-Presbyterian: 1650 W. Harrison Street, tel: 312-942-5000, www.rush.edu
University of Chicago Hospital: 901 E. 58th Street, Hyde Park, tel: 773-702-6250.

I

Internet

You will find that most hotels in the moderate to luxury categories provide internet access, usually in-room Wi-fi, but often for a fee. Large business hotels will also provide business centers with computers, printers, and office equipment for rent.

FedEx Office provide internet access and other computer, copy and mailing services for a fee. For a list of offices and hours, go to www.fedex. com/us/officeprint/main. Centrally located branches include those at 225 N. Michigan Avenue (tel: 312-819-0940 and 444 N. Wells Street (tel: 312-670-4460).

Every **Starbucks** is now a T-Mobile HotSpot, offering complimentary access to customers. **Barnes & Noble** stores provide free access as well. The **Chicago Public Library** system also provides free internet facilities:

Downtown: The Harold Washington Library, 400 S. State Street, tel: 312-747-4999

Lincoln Park: 1150 W. Fullerton Street, tel: 312-744-1926

Bucktown: 2056 Damen Avenue, tel: 312-744-6022.

M

Media

Print

The *Chicago Tribune* (www.chicagotribune.com) is Chicago's principal daily newspaper, one of the nation's largest dailies and the more conservative of the city's two major newspapers. The Tribune Company also owns WGN radio and television, which is named for the paper's original tagline, the 'World's Greatest Newspaper.'

The *Chicago Sun-Times* (www.suntimes.com) is Chicago's other daily paper of note and the oldest continually published one in the city. The paper was acquired by Canadian Conrad Black in 1994, who – along with his partner – was later indicted for fraudulent use of funds. After they were removed from the board, the publisher was purchased from now-deceased financier Jim Tyree and renamed the Sun-Times Media Group. Today, it stands as Chicago's more liberal, working-class newspaper.

Turn to *Chicago Reader* (www.chicagoreader.com), a free cultural and entertainment weekly, for local social and cultural, and political features. It's also a great source for concert, movie, theater, gallery, and stand-up comedy listings, as well as restaurant reviews and a weekly line-up of the best events in and around the city. Free copies are available at bars, coffee shops, delis, and bookstores throughout the city.

Time Out Chicago (http://timeoutchicago.com) is the local version of this multi-city, monthly magazine.

Chicago (www.chicagomag.com) is a monthly magazine published

by the Tribune Company, a go-to
for features and a resource for
real estate news. It also provides
information on shopping and home
and garden destinations as well as
the dining scene.

Television
WBBM Channel 2 (CBS)
WMAQ Channel 5 (NBC)
WLS Channel 7 (ABC)
WGN Channel 9 (WGN)
WTTW Channel 11 (PBS)
WCIU Channel 26
WFLD Channel 32 (Fox)
WSNS Channel 44 (Telemundo)
WPWR Channel 50
WGBO Channel 66 (Univision)

Radio Stations
News
WBBM 780 AM News Radio
WLS 890 AM News Talk
WSCR 670 AM Sports Radio
WVON 1450 AM News Talk
WGN 720 AM News Talk and Sports
WBEZ 91.5 FM Chicago Public Radio
WMVP 1000 AM Sports Radio

Music
WXRT 93.1 FM Rock
WLUP 97.9 FM Classic Rock
WKQX 101.1 FM News Talk
WTMX 101.9 FM Adult
Contemporary
WNUA 95.5 FM Spanish

Money
ATMs
ATMs are at banks, some stores, and

bars, and charge varying usage fees:
check also with your bank at home.

Currency
The dollar ($) is divided into 100
cents (¢). Common coins are the
penny (1¢), nickel (5¢), dime (10¢),
and quarter (25¢).
   Common bills are the $1, $5, $10,
$20, $50, and $100 bills.

Exchange
It's best to change foreign currency at
airports and major banks downtown.

Traveler's Checks
Banks, stores, restaurants, and hotels
generally accept traveler's checks in
US dollars.

P
Parking
Parking meters accept credit cards
and are generally limited to a
two-hour maximum; however, it's
important to note the cost for the
city's metered parking is ever on
the rise. Permit restrictions apply
in most neighborhoods; always
check the red-and-white signs that
designate parking restrictions
and tow zones, and look out for
temporary signs that indicate
street cleaning. Traffic police are
omnipresent and efficient, so it's best
not to take chances.
   On balance, parking garages are as
expensive as taxis: the average cost
of one to four hours is $19, while up

to 24 hours is $20–28. The best deals on parking downtown are probably at Millennium Park (South Columbus Drive between Monroe and Randolph streets) and Grant Park (Grant Park North Garage, Michigan Avenue, and Randolph Street; Grant Park South Garage, South Michigan Avenue between Jackson Boulevard and Van Buren Street).

Postal Services
Most post offices are open from 8.30am–5pm Monday–Friday and 8.30am–1pm Saturday. The post office at 540 N. Dearborn Street is also open Sunday 9am–2pm.

US Post Offices
100 W. Randolph Street, 60601
222 Merchandise Mart Plaza, Suite 102, 60654
540 N. Dearborn Street, 60610
358 W. Harrison Street, 60607
433 W. Van Buren Street, 60607
3024 N. Ashland Avenue, 60657
1343 W. Irving Park Road, 60613
2405 N. Sheffield Avenue, 60614

Public Holidays
The US has shifted most public holidays to the Monday closest to the actual dates, thereby creating a number of three-day weekends. Holidays that are observed no matter the day on which they fall are:
New Year's Day (January 1)
Independence Day (July 4)
Veterans' Day (November 11)
Christmas Day (December 25)

Other holidays are:
Martin Luther King Jr Day (third Mon in Jan)
President's Day (third Mon in Feb)
Memorial Day (last Mon in May)
Labor Day (first Mon in Sep)
Columbus Day (second Mon in Oct)
Election Day (first Tues in Nov, every four years)
Thanksgiving (fourth Thur in Nov)

R
Reservations
It is highly recommended that you book hotels well in advance, especially during the peak summer season (May through September) and holidays (Thanksgiving and Christmas). Good restaurants book up quickly on weekends, so always try to make a reservation at least a couple of weeks ahead of time. If you can't get a reservation, it's often worth arriving early, putting your name down, and having a few drinks at the bar; most restaurants keep a couple of tables open and dining in the bar is often a good fallback.

Architectural River Cruises are also extremely popular and sell out fast, as do tickets for Second City, Hubbard Street Dance, and the Joffrey Ballet.

T
Taxes
Hotel tax is 15.4 percent; sales tax is 9.75 percent; restaurant tax is 11 percent.

Telephones

Public phones accept coins and calling cards. The country code is 1. Chicago area codes are 312, 773, and 872 for the metropolitan area. Other useful codes include: 630 and 331 for western suburbs; 708 for south and near-west suburbs; 847 and 224 for north and northwest suburbs; and 815 and 779 for northwest and far southwest suburbs.

Telephone dialing cards, available widely in convenience stores and elsewhere, are an inexpensive way to make calls.

Directory enquiries: 411.
US calls outside your area code: 1 + area code + phone number
International calls: 011+ country code + phone number
Operator: 0 for assistance with local calls; 00 for international calls

Time Zones

Chicago is in the central time zone (-6 GMT). Daylight saving begins the first Sunday in April and ends the last Sunday in October. Flights from Australia and New Zealand cross the international date line; you will arrive in Chicago before you left home.

Tipping

Service personnel depend to a large extent on tips. Gratuities are expected at all full-service restaurants unless a 15–18 percent service charge has been added to your bill, as is often the case with parties of six or more.
Waiters: standard 18 percent, for exceptional service 20–25 percent
Doormen, bell boys, porters: $1–$2 per bag
Taxi Drivers: 10–15 percent
Hairdressers, manicurists, and masseurs: 20 percent
Valets: $3 per car
Chamber staff: discretionary according to standard of service and length of stay

Tourist Information

Chicago Cultural Center, 78 E. Washington Street, tel: 312-744-6630, www.cityofchicago.org/tourism
Chicago Office of Tourism, 163 E. Pearson Street, tel: 312 744 2400
Illinois Bureau of Commerce, James R. Thompson Center, 100 W. Randolph Street, tel: 312-814-7179, www.enjoyillinois.com

Transportation

The main forms of public transportation in the area – the Chicago Transit Authority (CTA), PACE buses and Metra trains – are overseen by the Regional Transportation Authority (RTA). It offers maps and trips on its website, www.rtachicago.com.

The 'L'

The 'L' (elevated train) is a rapid-transit system run by the CTA (tel: 312-836-7000; www.rtachicago.com). It consists of eight lines that serve downtown and outlying neighborhoods as well as a few suburbs. Service is generally efficient, although ongoing maintenance work on the tracks and structures can cause slowdowns during off-peak hours. The cost of a single ride is $2.25, and transfers to buses are 25 cents. You'll need to purchase a fare card with cash; they are available from machines at all stations. If you are planning on using the 'L' and buses extensively, consider investing in a one-, seven-, or 30-day pass.

Buses

The 'L' doesn't go everywhere, so buses come in handy. The network is extensive and somewhat confusing, so your best bet is to pick up a system map or check out the CTA website, www.transitchicago.com, which features an online trip planner. Get passes and fare cards at 'L' stations, Jewel and Dominick's grocery stores, CVS, Walgreens, and currency exchanges.

For travel beyond the reach of the CTA, you may end up transferring to a bus run by PACE, which services the suburbs (tel: 847-364-7223; www.pacebus.com).

Metra train

Metra trains are used mainly by commuters traveling to and from the suburbs, but they're another option when the 'L' doesn't serve your destination and a bus would take too long. Most of the lines arrive at and depart from Union Station (225 S. Canal Street; 312-322-6777) and the neighboring Ogilvie Transportation Center (tel: 312-496-4777; www.metrarail.com).

Cycling

Chicago is officially a bicycle-friendly city. Currently, there are 117 miles (188km) of on-street bike lanes and over 30 miles (48km) of marked shared lanes. There are also many off-street paths, including the scenic, 18.5-mile (30km) Lakefront Trail.

Taxis

Taxis can be hailed on the street or found at cabstands. The meter starts at $2.25 and goes up $0.20 cents for each ninth of a mile. There are additional charges for extra passengers.

W

Websites

The following sites contain a wealth of information on Chicago's cultural sites, history, politics, literature, sports, and entertainment:
www.centerstage.net
chicago.metromix.com
www.chicagoreader.com
www.choosechicago.com
www.cityofchicago.org
www.explorechicago.org
www.huffingtonpost.com/chicago
timeoutchicago.com

Blogs

blog.chicagoarchitecture.info
chicago.eater.com
www.chicagofoodies.com
www.chicagoist.com
www.chicagonow.com
www.thefeast.com/chicago
www.gapersblock.com

Index

Insight Select Guide: Chicago
Written by: Jennifer Olvera
Edited by: Sarah Sweeney
Layout by: Ian Spick
Maps: Stephen Ramsay and Apa Cartography Department
Picture Manager: Steven Lawrence
Series Editor: Carine Tracanelli

Photography: All Pictures APA David Dunai except: Alamy 12T, 79; Blue Chicago 58; Corbis 29; Getty Images 77, 110; Istockphoto 48, 70; Lill Street Art Center 28; Lincoln Park Zoo; Loupe 52; Museum of Contemporary Art/Stephen Hall; Photolibrary 3T, 4/5, 37, 80, 96, 98; Rex Features 76; Courtesy Skydeck 12B; Steppenwolf Theatre 54; Courtesy Vosges Haut Chocolate
Basemap data: on pp.20-1, 44-5, 122-3, 136-7, 154-5 derived from OpenStreetMap © OpenStreetMap and Contributors, CC-BY-SA

First Edition 2012
© 2012 Apa Publications UK Ltd.
Printed in Germany

Distribution:
Distributed in the UK and Ireland by:
Dorling Kindersley Ltd,
a Penguin Group company, 80 Strand, London, WC2R 0RL, UK;
email: customerservice@dk.com

Distributed in the United States by:
Ingram Publisher Services
1 Ingram Boulevard, PO Box 3006,
La Vergne, TN 37086-1986, USA;
email: customer.service@ingrampublisher services.com

Distributed in Australia by:
Universal Publishers
1 Waterloo Road, Macquarie Park, NSW 2113, Australia;
email: sales@universalpublishers.com.au

Worldwide distribution by:
APA Publications GmbH & Co. Verlag KG (Singapore branch)
7030 Ang Mo Kio Ave 5, 08-65 Northstar @ AMK, Singapore 569880;
email: apasin@signet.com.sg

Contacting the Editors
We would appreciate it if readers would alert us to outdated information by writing to:
Apa Publications, PO Box 7910, London SE1 1WE, UK;
email: insight@apaguide.co.uk

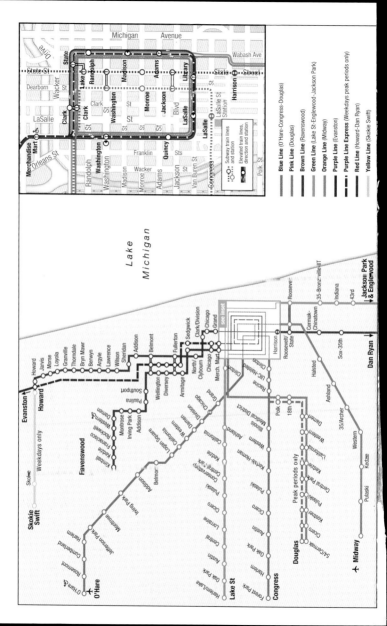

Michigan Avenue

State St

Dearborn

Wacker St

LaSalle

Clark

Merchandise Mart

Orleans St

Randolph
Washington
Madison
Monroe
Adams
Jackson

Franklin

Michigan Avenue

Wabash Ave

State Randolph
Lake
Washington
Madison
Monroe
Adams
Jackson
Library

Clark St
Washington St
Monroe St
Jackson Blvd
LaSalle St

State Street

LaSalle St Station

Harrison

Quincy Sts

Van Buren St

Congress

Polk St

Subway train lines
and station

Elevated train lines,
direction and station

Blue Line (O'Hare-Congress-Douglas)

Pink Line (Douglas)

Brown Line (Ravenswood)

Green Line (Lake St-Englewood-Jackson Park)

Orange Line (Midway)

Purple Line (Evanston)

Purple Line Express (Weekdays peak periods only)

Red Line (Howard-Dan Ryan)

Yellow Line (Skokie Swift)

Lake Michigan

Evanston
Howard
Jarvis
Morse
Loyola
Granville
Thorndale
Bryn Mawr
Berwyn
Argyle
Lawrence
Wilson
Sheridan
Addison
Belmont

Weekdays only

Skokie
Skokie Swift

Ravenswood

Kimball
Kedzie
Francisco
Rockwell
Western
Damen

Montrose
Irving Park
Addison

Southport
Paulina

Wellington
Diversey

Fullerton

Sedgwick
Clark/Division
Chicago
Grand

North/
Clybourn
Armitage

Chicago
Grand
Merch. Mart

Clinton

Red line inset

O'Hare
Rosemont
Cumberland
Harlem
Jefferson Park

Montrose
Irving Park
Addison

Logan Square
California

Western
Damen

Division
Chicago
Grand

Illinois
Medical District

Racine
UIC-Halsted

Clinton

Clinton
LaSalle
Roosevelt
State

Harrison

Roosevelt

35-Bronzeville-IIT

Indiana

43rd

Jackson Park
& Englewood

Cermak-
Chinatown

Sox-35th

Dan Ryan

Conservation/
Central Park

Kedzie
Kimball
Pulaski

Central Park
Kedzie

Kostner
Cicero
Pulaski
Central Park

California

Western
California

Ashland

Halsted

Polk
18th

Damen

Western

35/Archer

Kedzie

Pulaski

Midway

Peak periods only

Douglas

54/Cermak
Cicero
Kostner
Pulaski
Central Park

Harlem/Lake
Oak Park
Forest Park

Harlem
Oak Park
Austin
Central
Lorraine
Cicero
Pulaski

Kedzie
California
Western
Ashland

Lake St

Congress